Weapons and Warfare in the Zombie Apocalypse

Adam Alasdair, Ph.D.

ISBN-978-0988806122

-For anyone who has ever passed a building or a
piece of terrain and though to themselves, "I could
use that to defend myself against zombies..."

Excellent Book

Contents

A Note about the Apocalypse

This volume is dedicated to a study of weaponry and battle tactics as they specifically relate to an apocalyptic zombie outbreak. What exactly do I mean by "Zombie Apocalypse?" That's an interesting question. Certainly the lessons learned from reading this volume could be applied to other sorts of zombie epidemics. Locally, a large enough outbreak might even replicate many scenarios found in a true zombie apocalypse, even if society was elsewhere intact. But the true intent of this book is to prepare readers for a world-wide zombie pandemic. This specifically means a plague of zombies so large that nations around the world collapse and the living dead outnumber the living by a wide margin. In the hypothetical situation this volume assumes, after the initial destruction and devastation caused by the breakdown of societies around the globe, as much as 99% (or even more) of the world's human population has fallen victim to zombies or the fallout of the breakdown of civilization. The world inhabited by the relative handful of human survivors will be very different from that of the early twenty-first century that is our present. This is especially true in the so-called First World nations, whose relatively privileged and well-off inhabitants have the longest way to fall as civilization world-wide takes on many of the trappings of our medieval or ancient pasts. If you live in. Africa with only minimal access to electricity and running water, the new world of the apocalypse isn't going to be so different. Except for the ravenous walking corpses. But for the denizens of the wealthy countries of Europe or the United States the fall will be shocking and dramatic. It will also more than likely be the cause of greater loss of life, since the citizens of the First World mostly lack many of the basic survival skills that we've exchanged for our technologies and machines.

Much of this volume's content is directed at the citizens of the modern US. Certain sections, especially those related to firearms and ammunition, are designed to be of use by survivors who have access to the remnants of early twenty-first century America's gun culture. In much of the rest of the world these sections will be of only partial value, given the differences in the rates of gun ownership and the prevalence of firearms and ammunition. Other sections, such as those dealing with ancient or improvised weaponry, should be useful to survivors around the globe. So the advice contained herein has some utility no matter where you find yourself at the dawn of the new world—the world of the zombie—even though some of the content is biased in favor of American survivors. Fight well, and remember to always watch your back.

A Brief Introduction

When mankind stumbled upon agriculture at the end of the Neolithic period, it wasn't very long before he learned that taking things from others was easier than laboriously growing or making them himself. Thus warfare was born, and quickly resulted in the invention of all sorts of sophisticated and specialized technologies such as weaponry and defensive fortifications. Man is enormously inventive when it comes to figuring out how to kill his own kind (and members of pretty much every other species as well). Combined with our inventions, our intellect makes us the deadliest predator to ever walk the earth.

In the event of an apocalypse-level zombie epidemic, however, this may no longer hold true. Outwitted by the inexorable force of a microscopic pathogen (or space dust or however zombies come into being, for the purpose of this volume it really makes no difference), most members of our species would succumb to a threat that we can't beat with arms or intelligence. With the bulk of the human population transformed into ravenous automatons, the survivors will face a transformed world where most of the old patterns of existence no longer apply. There are myriad dangers survivors would face in this new world, and zombies are only one of these. The environment itself would quickly become an enemy as the electricity failed (if you live in the US you can thank all the people who don't want to pay taxes, because our tottering electrical grid is long overdue for a radical overhaul). Even in countries with better infrastructure, without human controllers most power would quickly vanish, taking artificial light and heat with it. Water supplies would become contaminated for the same reason, a situation exacerbated by the large numbers of unburied corpses that would be a feature of societal collapse. Food supplies might be largely looted or destroyed during the initial stages of the outbreak, as human populations became increasingly panicked. Food remaining in supermarkets would become prey to a variety of rodent and insect pests, while rotting vegetable and animal products would teem with bacteria, making the corner store a dangerous place. Fire would be an enemy, rather than an ally, as unattended pilot lights led to infernos in cities and suburbs. Reserves of pressurized natural gas could explode, further increasing the danger posed by fire. Around the world, nuclear power plants would eventually become grave threats to the regions surrounding them: without humans to maintain the coolant levels, spent fuel rods would inevitably cause thermonuclear explosions, poisoning the countryside in all directions with lethal amounts of radiation. Without modern medical technology, survivors would be suddenly thrust back in time to the medieval world, where otherwise minor illnesses or injuries could prove fatal. Obviously, the world of the zombie apocalypse is a dangerous place, even discounting the hordes of the walking dead. But there are a number of other manuals detailing these and other dangers, and the reader is encouraged to make every effort to seek them out. Preparation is the key to survival. This volume has a different, more specialized focus than the literature that currently exists on the subject of zombies and the potential breakdown of society that could occur following a world-wide zombie plague. It is important to remember what this manual is not, in other words. You will not find much information on food supplies or general scavenging here. There is no discussion of interpersonal relations beyond the requirements of armed combat. Absent is a conversation about long-term goals or travel or, for that matter, that much about zombies themselves. This book is not concerned so much with what created zombies but rather with how to engage them in battle. The focus here is warfare, from the point of view of a historian who has considerable knowledge of military history. It is a knowledge that is useful to apocalyptic survivors, and so I share it here with you. In the end I want you and yours not simply to survive—I want you go to war.

This book offers a discussion and analysis of weapons and warfare as these topics relate to surviving a world-wide outbreak of zombification. In the modern world the concept of self defense is taken seriously by certain individuals, but in reality (at least in the developed world) the risk of violence is quite low. Most people will go their entire lives without needing to defend themselves from violent attack. In the post-apocalypse, both zombies and hostile surviving humans will make self-defense a necessity. Everyone who lives past the end of the world will need to become a warrior. This book is designed to offer some instruction on the nature of weapons and warfare in relation to the threats faced by survivors in a changed world.

There are two general sections (or books) contained within this volume. The first contains a detailed overview of the tools needed to provide for personal safety in the event of a violent encounter with zombies (and to a lesser degree, other people). The second, shorter section deals with a discussion of some of the tactics needed to survive actual combat. Overall, this volume is designed as a supplement to the existing body of literature. It is not an extensive how-to manual, but rather a focused discussion of the tools and techniques needed to survive battle, and not meet a greasy and terrifying end accompanied by the gnashing of decaying teeth.

Book I

Preparation

It might be self-evident, but it bears remembering that zombies are not people. They might have once been people, but the creature they've become has a completely different set of capabilities and vulnerabilities. As it specifically relates to combat, it is crucial to remember that psychology will only effect the reader, and not the zombie. There are no psychological restraints for the zombie, and this is an advantage for it and a disadvantage for you. You will be scared, even terrified when facing zombies, because your brain has the capacity to anticipate the future and dread what might happen to you if those decaying limbs manage to grasp your hair or clothing. You can anticipate with horror what it might feel like, sound like, to have blackened, jagged teeth sink themselves into your flesh as you shriek and kick in a futile attempt to get away. You have the capacity for fear, and that can complicate your attempts to resist zombie attackers. In contrast, the zombie is incapable of fear. It does not feel pain. It cannot anticipate what might happen to it and react defensively. The differing psychology between the living and the living dead is an important consideration that should not be taken lightly.

In the history of warfare, from the first stone arrowheads to the use of atomic weapons capable of leveling cities, fear is an incredibly powerful tool for an aggressor. There is a reason that medieval warriors drank alcohol, screamed war cries, and even bit the rims of their shields like the Viking berserkers. These behaviors are all responses to the very real fear that humans instinctively feel when confronted with violence and the possibility of bodily harm. The conditioning and training of soldiers since ancient times is in part an attempt to control the response that people feel when confronted with danger. In a confrontation with zombies you will be afraid. They will not be.

The zombie's complete lack of fear changes how you approach the problem of defeating them in battle. Assault rifles, for example, often have the capacity for fully automatic fire, that is, the weapon cycles after every shot and fires continuously until the ammunition supply is exhausted. Soldiers in combat use this ability sparingly, because fully automatic fire would quickly run through the standard ammunition load carried by individual soldiers. Automatic fire is mostly reserved for what is known as suppressing fire, i.e. firing lots of bullets in the direction of a hostile enemy in order to get them to duck and cease their own fire. Obviously this is totally meaningless with zombies. They can't be suppressed, because they can't feel fear. Automatic fire should therefore be mostly discarded against undead foes, since all it would achieve is the squandering of ammunition reserves.

Zombies, being undead, cannot succumb to wounds as humans easily can. For a human (especially considering the post-apocalyptic dearth of good medical care) a gunshot or stab wound is extremely dangerous. Even a small-caliber bullet can easily sever major arteries, leading to loss of blood pressure, unconsciousness and death. The same bullet hitting organs like the kidneys or liver would result in much the same thing. Lungs can collapse. Piercing wounds to the lower abdomen carry with them the risk of infection and contamination by the bacteria of the digestive tract. Wounds to the heart are of course fatal, as are injuries blunt or otherwise to the brain or the spinal column. Even normally minor wounds to the extremities can prove fatal in the absence of medical care. The various types of gangrene are fatal if untreated, and offer a particularly gruesome fate. In short, humans are fragile sacks of meat with lots of vulnerabilities. Zombies have few of these limitations.

Zombies are immune to pain, which makes fighting one different from fighting a human. You cannot inflict a painful wound on a zombie in order to gain time to escape, or create an opening for another attack, as you can with a human opponent. You cannot debilitate a zombie through the use of pain. Moreover, zombies will not fall victim to blood loss, as a human opponent might following a wound that is not immediately fatal. Historically speaking, throughout human history most people killed on the field of battle were not killed outright: instead, they suffered one or more wounds that slowly killed them. After the battle of Waterloo in 1815, for example, thousands of wounded soldiers continued to die from their injuries for several months after the one-day battle was over. Zombies, in contrast to humans, cannot by definition be wounded, although their ability to function can be impaired if significant trauma is inflicted upon the body. The point to remember is that a zombie will not stop unless major damage is inflicted to the brain. Nothing else will completely stop them. Thus combatants encountering zombies need to modify their techniques to take into consideration the difference between the living and the undead.

Firstly, it should be remembered that while zombies are essentially super-human (or perhaps non-human) when it comes to fear or pain, they do have some of the same limitations that humans are constrained by. In terms of their physical structure they use the same musculature and skeletal system to provide for mobility. Just because they can't feel pain doesn't make their bones or muscles less susceptible to damage. This means that they can be slowed or crippled by damaging attacks to the extremities, which might be useful depending on the situation. Severing the vulnerable spinal column by cutting through the neck, or smashing it with a blunt instrument or bullet is a good way to stop a zombie: their vestigial brains depend upon the spinal column to relay information to the rest of body just like yours does, so the spine is a prime target for your attacks.

The main target, obviously, of any anti-zombie weapon is the brain that controls the creature's body. Everything you do to strike at a zombie comes down to destroying the brain or severing its connection with the rest of the body, in order to eliminate the threat presented by that body (note that severed zombie heads, or heads attached to crushed spinal columns might still be able to bite, so watch your step). Targeting the skull of a zombie, with the view of piercing through it to the vulnerable brain beneath is not as easy as it might appear. Remember that the skull is designed by nature to defend the brain at all costs. It is the hardest part of the human body for good reason. Especially when considering the use of hand-held weapons keep in mind that breaking through the defense offered by the skull may not be easy. You should always be prepared to strike again, until the creature stops moving.

This is obviously a brief overview of the biological constraints of zombies. I stress again that the reader should refer to more detailed discussions of the anatomy and physical capabilities of zombies found in other works. The survey above is meant as a sort of refresher course prior to the lengthier discussion of weaponry that commences below. In any event, with the dead far outnumbering the living, where they came from or why isn't in the end very useful information.

Improvised Weaponry

Sooner or later anyone facing zombie opponents is going to have to utilize everyday objects that are not normally considered to be or used as weapons. In fact, these items (and there's a bewildering variety of possibilities) are in general more common than firearms or other weapons and they are commonly encountered. Every household will certainly have something (and probably many somethings) that can be utilized as an anti-zombie weapon as the situation warrants it. Due to the inevitability of having to face a zombie armed with something that wasn't intended to be used in armed conflict, everyone should familiarize themselves with the basics of turning everyday objects from the environment into weapons.

The most obvious of these items are commonly employed around the house as tools. A partial sampling of such items might include the following:

Axes and hatchets- These items are intended to chop through saplings and branches, and to a lesser degree the chopping of fire wood and kindling. They come in a variety of sizes and weights and are more than capable of inflicting a fatal crushing blow to a zombie's skull. Axes were a fairly popular purpose-built weapon from antiquity through the European Middle Ages, since they were cheap and simple to manufacture. They were also quite good at piercing armor, although their weight and balance tended to make them less adaptable during combat when compared to swords. Note that axes and hatchets in your barn or garage (or your neighbor's barn or garage) are not the same as the medieval variants that were specifically designed for combat. The domestic axe is a tool, meant to be used against immobile, non-resisting timber. When used against lumbering zombies, keep in mind that the weight of axes, especially heavier models like fire axes, makes them poorly balanced as weapons. They are slow to recover from a missed strike. Also, missing the zombie means the chance of striking yourself with the axe blade, which is sufficient to cause a debilitating wound (leaving you slow or immobile and less able to escape the still-dangerous zombie). With these as with other weapons, they should be matched to your physical strength. If you have no choice and need to use it in a pinch, fine—but if the tool or weapon isn't effective given your level of physical strength, find something more appropriate as soon as possible.

Hammers and picks- Another excellent make-shift weapon against zombie attackers, hammers come in even greater variety than axes do. These are shorter weapons, obviously, than axes and therefore they necessitate that the user get dangerously close to a zombie foe. However, their weight and reach makes them relatively handy in close, and they have the ability to inflict a depressed skull fracture or pierce the skull. The claw end of the hammer has some of the characteristics of medieval war picks, although the point(s) are not nearly as acute as the medieval examples. Historically, war hammers and the related war picks were developed during the fourteenth and fifteenth centuries as a response to improved armor technology. Articulated plate armor was largely impervious to sword blows, because the glancing surface would cause attacks to slide harmlessly off. Even if an opponent managed to strike a hard blow with a sword, in general the solid plate that covered most of the body could not be cut or pierced by swords. Because of this, knights and other warriors began to carry axes and especially hammers and picks in addition to their other weapons. Upon encountering someone in full plate armor, the hammer or pick was deployed as an armor piercing weapon to bludgeon through the enemy's defense. Clearly, if the intent of such weapons was to inflict damage to someone wearing steel plate armor, then an unarmored zombie skull is relatively vulnerable to the piercing and hammering effect of such weapons.

Baseball/Cricket Bats- These are clubs, albeit specialized clubs used for organized sports. They can readily be turned into weapons in a pinch, as scared apartment dwellers and mob enforcers can attest. Clubs are one of the oldest forms of weapon, up there with stone spears and knives. Deadlier forms of club were created over the course of man's millennia-long pursuit of warfare. Often these were embellished with stone or metal spikes or blades in an attempt to make the weight and impact of the club do even more damage once it hit. Baseball or cricket bats need to break their way through the skull or crush the spinal column to be effective against zombies. They are capable of achieving this, but bear in mind that a certain amount of strength is required, and timing is important. Also keep in mind that wooden clubs can potentially break: baseball bats are designed, as you know, to hit baseballs, not skulls attached to the mass of a moving zombie. Using a tool for a task it isn't designed for is a recipe for the failure of that tool, and your anti-zombie bat might break at the handle (its weakest point) when delivering a hard blow. If you use a bat remember that if the weapon fails you need to be ready to flee or quickly locate an alternative implement before you become a hot lunch.

Screwdrivers- Good quality screwdrivers, whether Phillip's head or flat, can become effective stilettos in a pinch. If you're only familiar with the term stiletto in reference to shoes, the pointy heel in question is actually named after an even more pointy type of medieval dagger. Stilettos were narrow bladed weapons that usually lacked an edge, being entirely designed around the use of the needle-like point for thrusting. They could pierce through weak spots or gaps in armor, or they could be worn in a smaller form as civilian self-defense weapons. The idea is essentially to focus a lot of force on a small point, with the idea that the point with them pierce through the target. Screwdrivers are capable of serving in this role, though their effectiveness would be even greater if they were modified by sharpening the point to a more acute edge. When targeting a zombie with such a weapon the eye sockets are probably the best place to strike: remember that you're trying to get to the brain, and you don't want to risk your screwdriver skittering off the curved surface of the skull, leaving you vulnerable to a bite. Screwdrivers are close-range weapons that should only be used if nothing better can be found. Remember that the zombie's danger zone extends only a few feet in front of the creature, limited by the reach of its arms. By closing to strike with a screwdriver, you're entering that danger zone and potentially making yourself vulnerable.

Kitchen knives- Similar to the use of the screwdriver, the kitchen knife is a close-ranged weapon that should be used carefully and only if nothing better is available. The technique of using a kitchen knife is similar to that of screwdrivers. Primarily useful as a piercing weapon, the kitchen knife should be targeted at the eyes or the base of the skull in order to incapacitate the attacking zombie. Secondarily, if your knife is sharp enough you can use it to slice at your attacker, but remember that 1) an incapacitated zombie is still dangerous and 2) if you're using a knife you're within striking distance of the zombie's hands and jaws. Where knives are concerned the larger the better, in general, realizing that even the largest knife is not the most ideal weapon. Quality knives shouldn't break, but keep in mind that you're using it for something it really wasn't designed for. If you're in a fancy (or well stocked) kitchen you might find a cleaver. Used in a manner similar to the hatchets, the cleaver's strengths are its weight and sharp edge. A hard enough blow should be sufficient to cut through the skull, though like the knife its short reach places the user in some amount of danger.

Scissors- Most cheap scissors won't be much use against a zombie. But if you happen upon a high quality set of scissors, especially those meant to cut fabric, they can be pushed into service as a sort of stiletto. The ring-shaped handles can be used to secure a decent grip around the base, and the blades are capable of concentrating sufficient force on a small point, which means they can be used as piercing weapons. You're probably familiar with the possibility of using scissors as makeshift weapons, because of the presentation of such a scenario by Hollywood. Remember that zombies are not humans, and so "close" doesn't count: only the brain or the spinal column will do. You'll need to use significant force to make it happen with scissors, and like other short weapons you'll be in danger the whole time.

Table legs- Another form of club. Lighter and generally less effective than baseball bats (if it's heavier, great, but then you're going to have a hard time breaking it off the rest of the table). They're included here in part because pretty much every house or apartment has some of these inconspicuously holding up the furniture. If it's all you've got, it's better than nothing. Use it to find your way out as quickly as possible, so that you can locate something better to defend your flesh from hungry zombies (with an emphasis on the "as quickly as possible" bit).

Pans- The right pan can be a decent weapon, in an emergency. Especially high quality examples. Pans have mass and are resilient enough to survive multiple blows. Cast iron, while extremely heavy, is probably the most lethal of this category of improvised bludgeoner.

Dumbbells and other weights- Another regularly encountered item, these are similar to the cast iron pans mentioned above. It's all mass, and all about using that mass to crush the zombie's skull before he gets the upper hand. The variety of hand weight known as a "kettle bell" (give a shout out to Russia for the idea) could be a very capable close-in bashing weapon, provided you can get your hands on a light enough example. They look basically like a cannon ball with a cast loop-like handle attached to the top. Swing one with enough force and the right timing and you'll have pulp instead of a zombie.

Shovels- Finally a weapon with some reach. Shovels can be pressed into service as a type of pole arm: they allow the user to keep some distance between him or herself and the offending zombie, and they can be used to both bash and pierce. Remember that a shovel blade is not sharpened for battle, and it's not going to shear through a zombie skull like you think it might. But with the right strike in the right spot, you'll survive to live another day, and get or manufacture a more effective weapon.

Pitchforks- Pitchforks (and scythes) have a long history of being put to use in (mostly failed) peasant rebellions. The failed part comes in when you consider that the authorities, depending on the time period, had either plate armor and warhorses or firearms with which to put down the rebels. Luckily for you, zombies don't have any of these things, and so you won't be facing a cavalry charge or a fusillade of rifle fire as you stand ready with your trusty pitchfork. These items give you reach, and the formula for effective piercing applies: lots of force focused on a small point (actually several points). Pitchforks can also be used to pin or maneuver zombies, if such tactics become necessary: impale your victim and then control him by manipulating the handle. You won't destroy the zombie by this method, but you might allow an ally to get an opening to strike or give yourself time to run or get a better weapon. Keep in mind that the handle might break, and be prepared if that occurs.

Rebar & steel pipe- Building materials offer up a range of products that might be used in a pinch as makeshift clubs. A piece of iron pipe or a short length of rebar encountered at a construction site might be sufficient to save your life, so that you live to run/fight/starve for another day. The technique is obvious: you supply the force, it supplies the mass and transmits the force to the skull. Crush away.

The Halligan tool- The holy grail of improvised anti-zombie weaponry, in my humble (but educated) opinion. Usually found in the proximity of firefighters, the Halligan tool is sort of like the bastard stepchild of a Swiss Army Knife and a crowbar, which firefighters use to poke, prod, pry, smash and generally dislocate all manner of inanimate objects in the course of their firefighting duties. It combines the characteristics of a war pick with a short spear, and has the added benefit of being highly useful because of its regular "day job" utility as well. You may well need to do some breaking and entering, and a Halligan Tool is your ticket to a successful life of post-apocalyptic crime.

Crowbar- An obvious follow up to the Halligan Tool, a crowbar is a heavy steel tool designed to destroy things. The hammer builds. The crowbar smashes. A hard blow and you'll reduce the zombie's skull to nibblets. Keep in mind that this isn't a light weapon. To use it and recover in time you'll need decent physical strength. Like the Halligan Tool, the crowbar is a spork for the apocalypse: it does several jobs, and it does them pretty well.

The Chainsaw- I include this here in part because it is a staple of some zombie fiction, and has been held up as an improvised weapon by Hollywood. Obviously a chainsaw can be used as a weapon: in fact, they are quite dangerous to use, even if you're familiar with them. Loggers have been slicing themselves up (accidentally) with chainsaws for a long time. They'll easily tear through most of the things in your path (and you, if you're not careful). Movies probably portray the chainsaw as a weapon because they're scary and dramatic. In reality, this should be about the last thing you want to grab as a means of defending yourself. If you're trapped with nothing but a letter opener and a chainsaw, pick the chainsaw. Otherwise, get something less ridiculous. The chainsaw's strengths are also its main weaknesses, in a sense: it has the power to dismember a body, but it's going to spray bits of that body all over the place (read "you") in the process. The fact that zombies are infectious masses of dead tissue should make you think twice before you decide to frolic amongst the flying zombie bits. Chainsaws are heavy, so if you're not already pretty strong, don't bother to try and use one as a weapon. The torque from their operation makes them still more difficult to use against attacking zombies. They are extremely noisy, so if you haven't managed to alert every zombie in your immediate vicinity, well, you have now. They run on gasoline (or an oil/gas mixture) which means they can only be used as long as the fuel supply lasts. Essentially, chainsaws are terrible weapons. Leave them to the actors who are only pretending to fight zombies.

Weapon Crafting

Survivors of the zombie apocalypse are generally going to be people who think fast on their feet and react swiftly to changing circumstances. They are going to be resourceful. Good at applying varied knowledge to solve the tasks at hand. Up to this point the discussion of hand weapons has been focused on items that are improvised weapons, implements like shovels and wood axes that were not designed to harm the human body but which can be put to that task in an emergency. This section is about something different (and highly useful). It is about making your own weaponry from what you have at hand.

If you make your own weapons you're embarking on what is essentially a historical experiment. Back in Neolithic times the first weapons were made not by specialized craftsmen but by the individual. Making something that stabs, crushes, or slashes is a very old notion, useful for hunting, for self-defense, and for taking at spear-point the valuable items held by others (and, often, the others themselves). Against zombies, the ability to make lethal weaponry out of what's on hand at the moment is an enormously valuable skill. Not only will you be more likely to survive, but you'll make your ancient ancestors proud.

There is no excuse for being poorly armed in the zompocalypse. Even if you're alone in the woods there are things that can be fashioned with a few simple tools that can vastly increase your ability to fight back against the undead. In the urban spaces of towns and cities there are myriad possibilities for the savvy survivor, in terms of weapon-making. The sky is the limit, so to speak, and your main restriction is your imagination.

Home-improvement and hardware stores are the real post-apocalyptic goldmines as far as weapon crafting is concerned. If you've got access to one of the large home warehouse stores you've hit the jackpot. An enormous amount of useful items are contained within the walls of the large chain stores, and the majority of the material inside is very unlikely to be looted by other survivors due to weight restrictions. Most of the looting will have actually happened before the actual apocalypse itself, mind you. The looters who stripped all the local grocery stores as things began to fall apart will have mostly been eaten or otherwise killed by the time the dead have taken over. In the panicked days and weeks before the breakdown of society most fearful people would be moving about, taking only their most vital possessions. Grocery stores and gun stores might be looted. The local home-improvement superstore will probably be more or less intact. At any rate, if you can find one of these, you should be set.

Not only are hardware and home-improvement stores likely to contain capable improvised weapons, they are stockpiles of all manner of useful items that can be used to fashion weapons or improve existing tools. The end goal is simple—produce an implement that will allow you to effectively destroy the zombie brain and/or spinal column, or improve an improvised weapon so that it will accomplish the same goal more effectively. The basic history of ancient weaponry is instructive in this regard.

Spears, axes, and maces/clubs (as noted above) are effective weapons and are some of the earliest implements made by man. Even a simple hardwood shaft can be made into an effective weapon. If a knife is used to whittle a point onto one or both ends these can be then be fire-hardened. A spear made in such a way was called a "pill" in the European Middle Ages. These weapons aren't meant for long-term use or for that matter for going up against opponents wearing much in the way of body armor. But against unarmored (and slightly squishy) zombies a fire-hardened spear would make a decent weapon for hand to hand combat, one that could stab and also block, trip and bash with the shaft. Similarly, a length of rebar or pipe can be transformed into an effective stabbing weapon by grinding a rough point on one end. These make-shift implements would be durable and effective. Handles and grip surfaces can be fabricated with wood, cloth, tape, or wire. A lead pipe could be transformed into an effective close range weapon that would combine the characteristics of a mace and a short spear.

Blunt weapons are effective against zombies, so long as you target the brain or the spinal column. But you can make an average blunt instrument, like a baseball bat for example, more effective by the addition of metal reinforcements, spikes, or plates. Nails and screws found at most hardware stores can be pressed into service in this way. Lengths of barbed wire can be wound around the shaft of a bat or other club to provide limited piercing ability and reinforcement. If you want more "oomph" to your club or bat you can use long nails or even railroad spikes to turn a bat into a sort of war pick. Alternately, a knife blade (or several blades) can be affixed to a club to grant it the ability to cut and pierce rather effectively.

A shovel handle and a decent knife can be turned into an effective short pole arm. In the parlance of medieval Europe such a weapon would be called a "glaive," although historical versions would have a stouter blade and a longer haft. These weapons were issued to infantry for use against armored knights, and your make-shift pole arm is only meant to cut through zombie tissue. Spears can be manufactured in the same way. As long as you have a blade or a spike and something to affix it to, you should not be going about unarmed. There is no excuse for doing so. If you're a year into the zombie apocalypse and you're still carrying about the poker you grabbed from your neighbor's fireplace, then you're getting a failing grade in zombie survival. Remember, in the zompocalypse you're no longer an office worker or a teacher or a mailman. You're a warrior. You have no choice if you wish to live. And warriors need weapons. If you can't find a good sword, get a machete. If you can't get one of those grab a bat or a fire axe. If you've got down time, improve your weaponry to make it more effective.

Axes are one of the more interesting items to manipulate, so long as you've got an example with a decent blade (the cheapest axes are not made of high-grade steel). If you've still got electricity, find yourself a grinder. If you've got no electricity, find yourself a home improvement store and plan on taking a few days off. With a bag of concrete and some fine sand it is relatively easy to cast a grinding wheel that can be manipulated by hand or hooked to a simple foot pedal. Grinding wheels of this type were how most large bladed implements were sharpened prior to the adoption of electricity. Anyway, once you've rigged a grinding wheel all it takes is the application of a little patience and effort to grind excess metal off of an axe blade. Your goal is to transform your wood axe, a tool, into a variant of the medieval war axe, which was meant to cut flesh and bone, and not saplings or firewood. You'll need to keep some water on hand in order to cool the blade as you grind, because too much built up heat from friction will change the temper of the blade. The end result should have a slightly thick cutting edge, while the rest of the blade is considerably thinned. Looking at the blade from the top of the axe, you should see a lengthened diamond section (the blade) and then a thinning of the metal going back towards the socket of the axe head. The final product is much lighter than the mundane axes lying in shops and garages across the country. It is not meant to cut into fibrous, resilient material like wood. It is now specialized to perform one task: to efficiently hack through flesh and bone. Your new axe is much lighter and more agile in a fight. You can change direction to block or strike again much easier than before. A missed blow is less likely to carry on its forward momentum and harm you. All in all, you've turned a mundane improvised weapon into a deadly tool of war. This is the mindset of those who will survive the fall of civilization.

With a bit of imagination and a short length of chain you can manufacture a flail. Medieval flails came in a variety of styles and lengths. They were derived originally from grain flails, which could be pressed into service in their own right. When manufactured specifically for warfare the flail was a weapon that could crush through armor and wound or kill the warrior behind it. Flails worked by using a length of chain which acted as a hinge that magnified the force of a blow. As the weapon was swung the business end of the flail would snap around and deliver a brutal impact to the target. These weapons were often enhanced by the addition of spikes or other protrusions that added to the lethal effect of the weapon's strikes. They came in both single-handed and double-handed varieties, and both of these weapons could be made with a variety of materials at a decent hardware store. They would be more than capable of destroying a zombie's will to live. As with the originals, care should be taken not to swing the weapon into your own body. A rogue flail can easily be lethal to an unarmored human.

Your Arsenal: Preparation vs. Scavenging

Some of the extant literature on zombie preparedness argues for the stockpiling of tools and weapons in anticipation of the coming apocalypse. Some of this preparation is clearly good advice, especially where it concerns supplies of water and to a lesser extent food. The first step of survival is not dying of thirst in your apartment while the world falls apart outside. In terms of weaponry (both offensive and defensive) this advice can be good, as far as you don't take it too far. What good is stockpiling a magnificent arsenal, only to abandon it all when your house or apartment complex is overrun by zombies or bandits? When it is threatened by fire? Masses of equipment you can't carry with you do you now good. Excess baggage slows you down and makes you a target for the more unscrupulous survivors who would find it easier to kill you and take your stuff rather than procure their own. Thousands of rounds of ammunition you can't carry are useless to you in the long run. Zombies can break into most un-fortified structures if there are enough of them to work at it. They won't get tired trying to claw their way into Apartment B, while you huddle inside atop your pile of cartridge boxes. Starving or dying in a blaze of glory (and gnashing teeth) is much the same result, from your point of view. If you want to survive your weaponry needs to be portable. Think of yourself as a member of a sort of post-apocalyptic Special Forces group: you need to be agile and mobile and ready to move out on short notice. So don't burden yourself with unneeded gear, or an entire arsenal of weapons.

With the right mindset, and a practiced eye, you should be able to locate all sorts of useful items in the environment as you need them. Remember that with most of the population transformed into shambling zombies, there should be an abundance of weaponry available.

The availability of firearms has the potential to greatly increase your survivability. The availability of guns of course varies with your location, and in some countries they are going to be much rarer than in others. The modern US is literally drenched in firearms: there are between 250-300 million guns in private ownership in the US, which means that in the event of a zombie apocalypse you shouldn't have trouble locating something to shoot with. Owning guns in the US is a highly politicized issue, with masses of people supporting increased gun control from the political left, while an equally fanatical resistance pushes to uphold the rights of gun owners on the political right. Whichever end of the spectrum you place yourself on, if most people transform into undead cannibals you'll be happy to know that modern Americans are more or less surrounded by a sea of small arms and ammunition, of all types. In other countries, for example Britain or Japan, owning guns is far more restricted, to the extent that guns are almost nonexistent outside the ranks of the police or military. If you find yourself in one of these countries once the apocalypse happens, you'll have to do without firearms, for the most part. However you arm yourself, the focus of your attention should be a combination of mobility and offensive capability. Never forget that no matter how well you're armed you will inevitably be heavily outnumbered. You can't fight off hundreds or thousands of zombies by yourself no matter what tool you use. The numbers are very much on the side of the undead: they have millions and millions of reinforcements, all equally ready to rip you apart. The goal is not long-term victory, but rather the idea that you'll live to fight another day.

Now that we've covered in brief the concepts behind improvised weaponry, and the types of such weapons that can be identified in the environment, we'll move on to a discussion of purpose-built hand weaponry. These are actually more common that many people think, even though the designs of most of them stem from the medieval pasts of Europe, the Near East, China and Japan. We're not talking about antiques: in actual fact you want to avoid ransacking the local museum for whatever authentic equipment they might have. Iron weaponry doesn't last too well in the archaeological record, and many old swords and other weapons are fragile. You can relax, though, because there are plenty of manufacturers around the world that make perfectly serviceable swords and other weapons that would serve well should you need to use them to cleave through zombie skulls.

They are less commonly encountered than the tools and other items discussed above, obviously, but there are enough medieval and other weapons floating about to make an analysis of them worthwhile. Before we begin our survey of centuries-old fighting tools, the reader should consider a number of physical limitations regarding the use of ancient weapons.

A Note on Conditioning

Most modern humans are not in particularly good physical shape. If you've been in the US for the last couple of decades or so, you've probably noticed that our lifestyle has resulted in the population growing more and more obese. Simply put, we eat too much, too often, and when we do eat our food choices are mostly poor ones. We're fat and unhealthy, as a population. This is not good for us now, without the zombies. Add in the zombies and the fall of civilization and the unhealthy nature of the populace at large ceases to be simply a bad idea and becomes an outright liability. Even if you think the zombie apocalypse is unlikely to happen (shocking as such a thought might be), you should probably exercise more than you do.

If you intend to use medieval weaponry to defend yourself from zombies, note that these items will use muscles you didn't know you had, and they'll use them hard. Swords are heavy. Not heavy as in how Hollywood periodically portrays them, as in "too heavy to lift." Nor are they feather-light, which is the other mistake that movies make in regards to swords (especially) and other medieval weapons. Many films use swords with aluminum/alloy blades: these allow fast-paced fights, which audiences like, and prop swords are safer for the actors. But you need a real weapon, with the weight and resilience of a steel blade. The average single-handed sword (say, of the type used in twelfth-century Europe) will weigh somewhere in the neighborhood of 3-3.5lbs. To people who lift weights or frequent the gym, this will seem like a trivial amount of weight. Trust me, it is not. Not when you're in the process of swinging it around your body striking it into shambling corpses in a desperate bid to stay alive. Not when you're constantly fighting momentum in order to recover from a strike or reposition the weapon for another blow. Actually using a sword teaches you that they get heavy under use, and they get heavy fast. It would be a very good idea for you to strengthen your hands, forearms, and shoulder muscles in preparation for close combat with zombies. As a matter of fact, it couldn't hurt to make sure your legs and abdominal muscles are likewise prepared to fight. Basically, you should work out more than you do. Now, let's commence with a discussion of the available tools.

Maces, Hammers and Picks

These are going to be less commonly encountered than swords, but they are valuable weapons for someone with the physical preparation to use one effectively. Clubs and maces are some of the oldest weapons known to man. Egyptian pharaohs, for example, are commonly depicted "smiting" the enemies of Egypt in a stylized portrayal that invariably includes a mace. In these depictions, a giant-sized pharaoh (emphasizing his importance and semi-divine status) towers over a defeated enemy, sometimes grasping the head or hair of the victim, while brandishing a mace above his head. These images date at least to the second millennium BCE, so maces are clearly venerable bits of technology.

Maces have a lot going for them in terms of applying them against the threat of undead attackers. Their weight makes them useful, obviously, for crushing through the armor-like human skull. Being heavy, blunt instruments, they are difficult to damage, unlike swords. The maces that you're likely to encounter as reproductions will all more or less be based on extant examples from the European Middle Ages. These weapons were most popular during the late medieval period when plate armor made the wealthiest warriors essentially immune to sword blades. Steel maces were one of the weapons devised to crack open the armor plate of knights. Since these devices were designed to crush through plate armor (and hopefully, crush the man protected by the plate armor) you are unlikely to damage your mace even after repeated contact with zombie skulls. This resilience is nothing to be sneezed at: a good weapon needs to be reliable, and a mace is going to be able to give you good and loyal service for a long time. War hammers are also manufactured as reproduction weapons, and like maces these items would be excellent choices for use against hungry zombies. Like the mace, the war hammer was designed to crack open plate armor, so a skull should be no problem, again provided you've got the physical strength to be effective. Often war hammers were double-faced weapons, with a hammer on one end and a long spike directly opposite. This allowed the warrior to reverse the weapon and strike with all the mass of the hammer behind an acute point, which made the weapon capable of punching holes through armor plate. Be aware that "hooking" your zombie with a long armor-piercing spike can potentially trap your weapon, or rip it from your hand as the zombie falls. This general advice should be applied to all piercing weapons, whatever their origin: eventually, you will manage to get your weapon stuck in the body of your last opponent, so be prepared for this eventuality.

Swords

These are by far the most commonly reproduced medieval and early-modern weapon. They come in a bewildering variety of styles, though most of the more exotic ones will be found only in museums. In general, the most common sword types are those created during the medieval periods of Europe, Asia and the Middle East, and to a lesser extent early-modern Europe. I'll begin with an overview of the general type, and move to a more specific discussion of individual specimens and their utility. Firstly, remember that swords are meant to do two different things. One is to pierce, with a sharpened point, and the other is to hack, slash, or cut (there is a difference). Some swords were designed to do both, while others specialized in one or the other type of attack. The distinction between the two different types of sword is actually quite ancient. It predates the discovery of iron technology and was developed by the craftsmen who made the very first viable swords, which were made out of bronze. Both in the Fertile Crescent (modern Iraq, Syria, Lebanon, and Israel/Palestine) and in Europe, bronze swords were made to either cut or pierce, but not usually both. The problem with bronze is that the metal is softer than steel and doesn't take as sharp an edge. To reinforce bronze blades to make them capable of withstanding the forces of a slashing blow, the blade has to be reinforced with a thick ridge or spine, which in turn reduced the effectiveness of slashing attacks. Making bronze swords optimized for stabbing or piercing attacks means a narrow blade that is vulnerable to breaking. Bronze technology made the sword. Iron technology made it better.

About the year 1,000 BCE in the Eastern Mediterranean, bronze technology began to be challenged by the new "upstart" weapons made of iron. Iron had a number of advantages: most especially, iron ore was very much more common than bronze, which was an alloy of copper and relatively rare tin. Disrupt trade routes, and tin became difficult to find, which made bronze impossible to manufacture. The switch to iron weapons didn't happen overnight, in part because the technology of iron had to be perfected by trial and error. At first, iron weapons were no better than bronze, because of inferior manufacturing techniques, and the lack of knowledge about how to turn the new material into a truly effective weapon. However, over time iron weapons and tools became more and more effective, and eventually iron weapons could be made that were stronger and more effective than bronze, at a cheaper price. No long distance merchant activity was necessary once you had the requisite technology: hot enough fires and a means to introduce carbon to your iron ore meant that you could forge items in steel (iron with added carbon), which was a far superior material with which to construct a sword, or any other hand weapon. Once iron was discovered, bronze was on the way out (except for armor, where it was easier to work into complex shapes).

Iron swords tended to be relatively short weapons, at least at first. While bronze swords were cast in molds and emerged (after cooling) fully formed, iron had to be worked by hand. The process was more technically complex and required a long period of trial and error for people to perfect it. Shorter sword blades were easier to manufacture and the shapes were more forgiving to the smith. Basically, it takes more skill and better quality iron to produce a reliable long blade from iron. Longer blades were affected by more stress during use, and could snap or bend if the materials and workmanship weren't exactly right. Thus for a long time battlefields were dominated by rather short weapons than tended to be used for stabbing as much as cutting.

The classic example of this sort of weapon is the well known (for an ancient weapon) Roman gladius. Gladius means simply "sword"...the technical term during most of Rome's history was *gladius hispaniensis*, or "Spanish sword," which tells you something both about Roman imperial expansion as well as the openness of the Romans to adopting effective technologies from outside Italy. The gladius varied somewhat in terms of blade design over the centuries, but the changes were relatively slight and the weapon itself was used with the same techniques for hundreds of years. The blade was roughly twenty inches in length and about two inches wide, with a "diamond" blade cross section. Seen from the point the blade shape looked like a (highly flattened) diamond, with a pronounced central ridge that made the blade stiff. This meant that it was very effective as a stabbing weapon, a feature of the blade that the Romans made much of. While it was an excellent instrument for piercing, the width and weight of the blade made it quite effective at cutting as well. The hilts of Roman swords had only wooden or bone components, with no heavy pommel at the base to counterbalance the weight of the blade (as with later medieval weaponry). This meant that a gladius was somewhat blade heavy, increasing the power of cutting attacks. At the same time, the relatively light weight of the weapon made it lively in the hand, and easy to carry.

Against zombie opponents, the piercing effectiveness of the gladius combined with its impressive cutting stroke makes the weapon a good choice for self-defense. It is also light and compact enough to stay out of the way until it is needed. The limitation of the gladius, like most hand weapons, is that you're going to be close enough to an individual zombie to be in its danger zone, the area it can reach with its arms. That said, a gladius is a lot better weapon than something shorter, such as a knife. The weight of the weapon makes it effective at piercing and cutting, and it would be capable of severing the neck if kept well-honed. Modern swords (this goes for all reproduction blades from quality manufacturers) benefit from advanced industrial grade steels. This means that a fairly inexpensive reproduction gladius is going to have a high-quality blade, better than most ancient examples where smiths had to rely upon intuition and guesswork concerning the chemical properties of the ore they manipulated. Reproduction gladii (pl. of gladius) are stout weapons that have strong, rigid blades capable of taking a considerable amount of punishment. The fact that these weapons were intended to pierce armor, if necessary, makes them more than adequate to chop up walking corpses.

The gladius gradually evolved by the late Roman period (c. 250-450 CE) into a longer sword known as a "spatha." These weapons were in part influenced by the longer Celtic slashing swords that the Romans had encountered during their conquest of Gaul in the late first century BCE. The reasons for the transformation were complex, and caused by a mixture of cultural forces, tactical changes in combat, and technical expertise. Longer weapons were more difficult to forge than shorter ones, and so metallurgy and metalworking skills needed to be developed to a point where making long swords was feasible. What constitutes a "sword" is also something that is culturally determined—as with other aspects of warfare it is embedded in culture and therefore it changes as culture does. The influx of Celtic and Germanic peoples into the Roman state gradually influenced the Roman military system. By the late Roman period most of the warriors fighting in the Western Empire's armies were Germans. Tactical considerations were also at work, since Rome's enemies were either dispersed raiding bands or cavalry forces that could move rapidly. The Roman military responded to this development by adding more and more cavalry into its own forces, so that the cream of the late Roman army was no longer composed of heavy infantry as it had been in earlier times, but was represented by heavily armed and armored horsemen. A longer sword like the spatha was a much better cavalry weapon than the gladius, because the greater length of the spatha added to a soldier's reach while he was on horseback and allowed more powerful slashing attacks due to the momentum of the heavier blade. When the Roman epoch evolved into the early medieval period, these changes were carried onwards and continued by the new kingdoms that sprouted on the corpse of the Roman state.

The medieval European sword was generally a long slashing weapon with a blade between 30"-36" in length. The heavier blade was counterbalanced with a weighted pommel, with the balance point somewhat in front of the horizontal crossguard that protected the wielder's hand. The weapons varied to an extent over the centuries that we consider "medieval," but there were several basic types that can be considered iconic. Early in the medieval period so-called "Viking" swords were more or less directly descended from swords of the late Roman period. These had broad blades with a rounded cutting point, and are almost all distinguished by a broad "fuller," a shallow groove that ran the length of the blade nearly to the tip of the sword. These were not "blood grooves" as they are sometimes considered, but rather they served to lighten the blade while at the same time resulting in a strong and flexible weapon. Early medieval swords of this type were fearsome weapons capable of inflicting incredible wounds on the human body. They excelled at hacking and cutting attacks, which the rounded point served to enhance. Because of the blade shape, Viking-type swords have an effective cutting surface equal to that of a longer sword (the "sweet spot" of the blade where cutting is most effective is enhanced by the rounded point of the sword). They were also capable of very effective piercing strikes. Only in later times with the arrival of plate armor did swords evolve drastically acute points and rigid diamond-shaped blades which enhanced stabbing attacks. For most of the medieval period swords were multi-purpose weapons capable of stabbing and cutting. Any of the swords from the European medieval period would be excellent weapons for use against zombie opponents, seeing that zombies don't generally come equipped with armor.

The ferocious capacity of medieval swords to inflict wounds on the human body is dramatically shown in the skeletal remains of medieval warriors. One of the best-known examples of this comes from the graves of men killed during the fourteenth century battle of Visby on the island of Gotland, off the coast of Sweden in the Baltic Sea. The dead from that battle had arms and legs completely severed, gruesome piercing and cutting wounds that penetrated the skulls of many victims, and at least one example of an individual who apparently lost both of his legs to a single blow. The battle provides very graphic evidence of what medieval weapons can do to the human body.

Any medieval long sword would be a fine weapon to use against zombie opponents. They are more than capable of severing limbs to incapacitate zombies, and their blades can stab through, crush or sever the human head without too much trouble. There is a reason why medieval warriors used shields and wore armor: without it, you were just waiting for someone to come over and fillet you. Zombies, of course, don't have shields and don't wear armor, which means they're just moving sacks of meat waiting to be carved apart by your weapon. Note that the familiar cautions apply to medieval European swords as with other ancient weapons: they force you to get close to your opponent, which is dangerous, and they require physical strength and conditioning that modern people generally don't possess. Despite what Hollywood movies would have you believe, people can't just pick up swords and instantly become capable fighters. Medieval warriors were essentially a caste of professional soldiers (knights and their retainers, mostly) who fought for a living and practiced for war throughout their lives. An office cubicle is not a good training ground for medieval hand-to-hand combat.

Medieval swords are surprising versatile weapons. They can stab and cut efficiently, even with a relatively dull blade. If the lower portion of the blade is kept unsharpened they can be gripped by the blade in order to shorten the weapon or apply more force for a thrusting attack (this was common in the late medieval period when armor grew heavier). I recommend this "half-swording" technique for pretty much all swords carried for use against zombies. The ability to shorten the weapon and use both hands to accurately stab is more valuable to you than having a blade sharpened for its entire length. The point of the weapon and the point of percussion should be kept sharp, but the first ten or twelve inches of blade may be left rather dull. Beyond the blade the crossguard provides protection to the hand and can be used as a weapon at close ranges, as can the pommel. Striking a zombie's head with the pommel should crack through the skull if sufficient force is supplied, and this allows you to defend yourself at close distances where effective cutting is impossible.

Reproductions of medieval swords cover the full range of historical types. If you have a choice, some selection may be in order. For starters, the twelfth and thirteenth century European swords with very long blades were really meant to be cavalry weapons, used from horseback. If the blade is much longer than about 31" it was probably meant to be used by a mounted warrior. These weapons are incredibly effective from horseback— the long blade allows you to reach foot soldiers and the added momentum of the mount makes really powerful blows possible. The power generated was enough to slash through body armor. The problem for you is that the long bladed weapons are slightly less handy on foot and your main opponents— zombies—don't strap on mail armor. Speed and weight are issues, just as will all your other equipment. Therefore smaller, lighter weapons are probably a better idea than the full sized cavalry swords.

Viking-era (c. 800-1100 CE) designs are a good compromise between older Roman-style cut and thrust swords and the weapons of the High Medieval period (c. 1100-1300 CE). Despite the reputation of medieval Scandinavians (*vikngr*, or "Viking" means something similar to "pirate") as bloodthirsty barbarians, their military and other technology was actually quite sophisticated. Their swords, especially, were extremely well designed. The typical Viking-era sword has a relatively short blade between 29" and 31" in length, with a pronounced fuller meant to lighten the blade. They have hefty metal pommels which act to counterbalance the blade, so that while they have strong "blade presence" they are neither heavy nor clumsy. They are quite capable of effective stabbing, especially against semi-decayed zombie enemies, and their blade profiles allow them to inflict incredible cutting blows. Moreover, Viking swords are relatively lightweight. They combine great effectiveness with portability. They were designed for warriors fighting on foot, as you will be. A good Viking sword will not let you down.

Swords were used by Europeans on the battlefield until well into the twentieth century. Their final forms were more or less codified during the period of the Napoleonic Wars (1803-1815 CE), which was the last true heyday of commonly using cold steel for attack and defense. This was because smoothbore muskets had such limited range, accuracy and rate of fire that is was possible to survive an enemy's fire and make it to close range. Similar tactics used later in the US Civil War were far less effective, as attackers had to go through heavier and more accurate defensive fire for a longer period before they could come to grips with an opponent. During the Napoleonic Wars infantrymen and especially cavalrymen used a variety of swords on the battlefield, though the musket had come to be the dominant weapon.

The form these weapons took was only somewhat related to the earlier weapon developments of the medieval period. In general cavalry weapons were used more seriously and more often than were infantry swords, and they came in two basic types: long-bladed swords predominantly meant for thrusting, and curve-bladed sabers whose main purpose was to deliver a strong cut. Both were deadly weapons, and both types had detractors and supporters who fervently championed one style of blade over the other. In general the English tended to favor heavy cutting sabers, proclaiming that the wounds inflicted by these weapons were devastating to the victim and terrifying to his comrades. The French were somewhat more likely to advocate the use of stabbing swords, especially for the heavy cavalry. The argument favored by the French was that such swords could inflict a deep penetrating thrust that would invariably prove fatal. While the cutting blows of sabers were impressive and scary looking, they were less likely to kill the victim. The fact is that both types were deadly weapons, and both types were used in some combination by all armies. The tendency of soldiers of the day to be lax about sharpening their swords reduced the effectiveness of sabers (exacerbated by steel scabbards which dulled the blades they carried), but even a dull saber could kill, especially if the blow were dealt at speed from horseback.

These later European swords would be decent weapons to use against zombies. They have long blades, most of them being cavalry weapons, and they are not light. But the mass of their blades would readily cleave through squishy zombie parts, especially if they were kept diligently sharp. European sabers and thrusting swords provide more protection to the hand, since in the time they were used the wearing of personal armor had vanished except for a small number of specialized heavy cavalry who wore helmets and breast-and-back plate armor. The hilt bars of such weapons can be used as bludgeoning weapons at close range, and the unsharpened back edges (generally these are single-edged swords) allow the user the ability to grasp the blade with a second hand. They are effective and battle proven weapons that would be a decent addition to an anti-zombie arsenal. I myself own a French 1805 pattern light cavalry saber (a reproduction) which would be a fine weapon to turn against the undead. It has a great deal of blade presence and a stout heavy blade that can make very strong cuts. Despite the deep curvature of the blade it is also capable of thrusting attacks. They are well designed implements of destruction.

Another class of European swords deserves a brief mention here. These are the dueling swords that developed first in Italy and Spain during the Renaissance (c. 1300-1700) and gradually became the civilian "smallsword" that was still around as a dueling weapon in Napoleonic times. The rapiers that began this lineage were thrusting swords with extremely long blades. They were used in civilian duels in conjunction with parrying daggers or other defensive items, with the sword purely dedicated to attack. Attacks were made by thrusting, and the acute points concentrated a lot of force on a very small area. Complex systems of training developed and sword masters and training schools proliferated to train aristocrats in the art of fencing with these long stabbing swords. Over time the weapons grew shorter and lighter, eventually losing all vestiges of a blade edge to become purely thrusting weapons. The smallsword was the apogee of this development, with a square or triangular cross section that was incapable of holding an edge. The strength and rigidity of their blades meant that they could parry attacks on their own. Thus the armed civilian could carry a lightweight blade that would provide for both attack and defense. They are elegant and attractive little weapons that are an important part of the history of swords.

In my opinion neither the rapier nor the smallsword is an ideal weapon for use against zombies. The rapier is overly long and potentially an encumbrance that inhibits rapid flight. They are more or less useless at close range, given that only the tip is ideal for piercing a zombie's skull.

Essentially they are simply too specialized. A Viking sword can bash, stab, hack and cut at a variety of ranges. The rapier is a long range weapon limited to thrusting. The smallsword is generally a handier weapon, but it too can only stab. Their thin blades are more resilient than many people think they are, but there is still the chance that a falling body will rip the sword from your grasp, or deform the blade enough as it falls to snap it. These dueling weapons were not meant for the battlefield, but for the much more specialized realm of the civilian duel. Since you'll be fighting multiple opponents at a variety of ranges, I suggest choosing something else if you've determined to make yourself into a post-apocalyptic swordsman or swordswoman.

You are not required, of course, to limit yourself to European sword types once the zombies descend. You can scavenge (or purchase in advance) a wide variety of non-European swords that would be excellent zombie choppers. Probably one of the most common of these types are the famous Japanese swords linked with the bushi (warriors of the samurai class) who used them in feudal Japan. The most well known term for these is "katana," although that term simply means a sword with a moderately long blade and specific hilt construction and method of carry. Japanese swords came in a variety of lengths, from large daggers all the way up to great swords the height of a man. The medium-length sidearm sword is one you'll encounter the most in the US: the shorter "wakazashi" and the longer "katana." A variety of companies make or import these weapons, many of them mass produced with modern steels in China and Taiwan. The quality of these "Japanese" swords varies wildly. The best are probably the ones made by Japan's remaining master sword smiths, who have an accumulated mass of expert knowledge. The problem is that these perfect-quality weapons are very rare in the US and extremely expensive, costing in the thousands of dollars. There are some high quality swords made by American smiths, or higher quality examples imported into the US by companies interested in quality and not shy about charging premium prices. In general, modern steel is quite uniform and strong even on cheaper weapons. The weak spots on "garbage" swords (meant only as decorations) will be the hilt attachments and the link between the blade and the tang, the metal shaft contained underneath the hilt. Some of these may be case hardened, or made with alloy blades. Such "swords" are so in name only. But many inexpensive swords are real weapons, made of good carbon steel.

You won't need a masterpiece weapon (even if you could find one) to make effective use of a Japanese sword. Japanese swords are cut and thrust weapons, with a single curved cutting edge and an acute and very well-reinforced point. Contrary to the characterization of Japanese swords as purely cutting weapons, they are in fact more than capable of piercing mail and even lighter plate armor with their wickedly sharp points. If properly sharpened, the blade geometry of Japanese sword allows one to draw the blade along a target at the moment it is struck, increasing the cutting ability of the sword. Longer Japanese swords are intended to be used with two hands, the right hand always under the round "tsuba" (or hilt) and the left hand gripping the hilt further down and acting to pull the weapon through a target. To be really effective, you need both training and practice. Japanese swordplay is complicated (but then that's true of every sword in every culture) and is certainly not simply swinging a blade around like a baseball bat. Practice makes perfect, and you'll need to really contemplate the process of manipulating your blade to make attacks and recover to strike again. On the other hand zombies have a monotonous fighting style and they don't have weapons beyond their teeth. You won't be fighting a duel with angry samurai, so you can probably get by with being self-trained. As with the above, if you intend to make yourself in a lone swordsperson, spend some time while the internet is still up to do some more specialized study than I have time to deal with here.

Another common type of sword encountered in the US is a weapon of Nepalese origin, the kukri or khukuri. These blades are the traditional/national weapons of the Gurka warriors who have fought for the British since the nineteenth century. They have a distinctive blade form that is reminiscent of (and possibly derived from) swords dating back to the Greco-Roman period that had similarly forward curving blades. The kukri curves sharply forward, with the blade swelling as it curves outwards. Though these are compact weapons they are capable of really ferocious cutting blows, with the forward curve and the weight of the blade powering through tissue and bone. I include the kukri in this discussion of swords in part because the Gurka themselves seem to consider it to be a type of sword. Certainly when compared to pocket knives and so on a kukri is an impressive-looking implement. They would be excellent weapons to wield against a band of zombies. The blades are compact enough to make toting them around easy, and they can still cut and stab with great power. They can be reversed to pound or bludgeon with the heavy blade spine, and the designs have stout hilts with handle scales usually made from buffalo horn. These are not elegant weapons, but they are brutally effective, and are still carried by Gurka soldiers today.

The swords of the Middle East are an interesting blend of traditions. Arabian swords in pre-Muslim times (before the seventh century CE) where long bladed cut and thrust swords with distinctive hilt designs. You won't be encountering any of these as reproductions. Well into the period of the Crusades Islamic swords were predominantly straight bladed cutting weapons. It was only after the intrusion of Turkic and Mongol peoples from Asia (beginning in the eleventh century CE) that the curved-bladed scimitar (or shamshir) developed. These curved swords were fantastic weapons for mounted warriors, and remained in use for centuries. The curved sabers wielded by Napoleonic cavalrymen were actually derived from these eastern weapons, via central Europe due to

Turkish advances in the seventeenth and eighteenth centuries. Indeed, the dress sword used by US Marines is actually a late period scimitar based on weapons used during the Barbary War (1801-1805) in North Africa. Similar to a Japanese sword a good scimitar is a fine weapon. Like the Japanese version they are more than simply cutting weapons, although they are excellent at cutting and slicing attacks. Despite a heavily curved blade they are capable of piercing attacks, with the blade being more or less "hooked" into an opponent. They are reasonably compact and are generally light. A scimitar should be kept sharp, especially at its point of percussion, but if this is done it will perform admirably.

In summary a descent sword is an excellent weapon against the undead. They have reasonable reach, they can incapacitate your opponent quickly, and they do not run out of ammunition. If you can spare the weight of a sword it will prove to be an excellent tool in your fight for survival. They are not superweapons, and they have a number of definite limitations that need to be taken into consideration (more on this in the section of tactics). But it's hard to go wrong with a good sword.

Exotic Slaughter: The Katar

While I was in the process of finishing this volume an acquaintance of mine pointed out to me that a katar would be an excellent weapon against zombies. At first I thought he said "guitar," and so I replied, "yes, I suppose, they're made of hardwood, a steel bar reinforces the neck..." (at least in electric guitars). But no...my friend said Katar, rather than guitar, and he is absolutely correct—they would be good weapons for close combat against the undead. So this section is dedicated to this good advice, which was freely offered and quite appreciated. Thank you, sir.

Most people are more or less familiar with knives and swords, but the same can't be said for the katar. At least here in the US. In South Asia I'm betting that it would be rather well known. So what is a katar, you ask? Let me tell you.

The katar originated in medieval India. In appearance it looks like a gigantic punch dagger, with a tapered blade between one and three feet in length. The primary difference between a katar and other types of daggers and short swords is that the hilt of the katar consists of two metal bars and handle that sets perpendicular to the blade. The whole hilt looks sort of a like a steel letter "H" with the blade attached to one end. When gripped in the hand, the blade projects forwards from the knuckles, while the two metal bars extending back from the blade rest along the user's forearm. This makes the katar a very steady weapon, as it is sort of locked to the arm of its wielder.

In India and South Asia the katar developed into something of a status symbol, as well as being a battlefield weapon. Like the Indonesian kris dagger or the Japanese katana, it was associated with wealth, nobility and prestige. But it was also a deadly weapon. Katars were even used by particularly brave individuals to hunt tigers—if you could kill a tiger with what amounts to a large dagger, nobody was apt to question your resolve.

The katar's strengths were demonstrated on medieval Indian battlefields, and these same strengths would serve you well in the apocalypse. The blade of a katar is usually constructed with a reinforcing ridge that runs the center of the blade (giving them at least a partial "diamond" cross-section). This made the blades quite stiff and specialized to engage in the thrusting attacks that the katar was designed around. Katars are capable of inflicting tremendous blows, despite their relatively small size. This is because the design of the weapon focuses all the force of the user's shoulders (and some of his body weight) on the piercing action of the point. Katars were meant to punch through mail and even plate body armor, and their popularity is proof that they did this job well.

The great thing about zombies is that they don't wear body armor. A katar, you see, is meant to punch through the armor of an enemy and gut the man behind the metal. Without armor zombies aren't going to resist the thrusts of a katar very well. Simply thrust your trusty katar through an eye socket, or even through the front of the skull, and you should be happy with the results. The bars of the hilt can be used defensively, as well, and a leather-gloved hand wielding a katar should be well-armored against zombie bites. If you want to emulate some of the Sikh warriors of medieval India, you can even carry two of them, and wield one in each hand.

The only problem with the katar is that you're unlikely to find one once the apocalypse begins. After the order-anything-you-want feature of modern society vanishes, you're not going to have ready access to mass-produced katars. But you do have the option of making your own (hmmm...intriguing).

Before you protest that you don't know anything about blacksmithing or forge-welding, relax. You'll have lots of time to learn new things. There won't be any internet in the zompocalypse, and we'll all be suffering withdrawal symptoms. Anyway, making a functional katar is not so difficult as you might assume. Many of the original katars were themselves made with broken sword blades, a form of useful recycling of still-usable metal. Any large knife or dagger could be pressed into service to provide you with a blade for your katar. Optionally, you could endeavor to learn some basic smithing so that you make your own from scratch—it doesn't have to be artwork, remember, you'll only be piercing zombies with it. Railroad spikes are one source of metal for your smithing pursuits, although to be fair they're usually made of lower carbon steel than what would be ideal. But again, you'll have time on your hands.

If you can at least learn some forge-welding techniques, you'll be able to press a pre-made steel blade into service and weld it to some iron to form a handle (remember the handy hardware store?). This is obviously an endeavor that takes more skill and effort than picking up a random machete, but it might be worth it in the long run. If you manage to make a katar or two for yourself, you're definitely getting an "A" in zombie survival. As an added benefit, anyone you come across is going to know you mean business. Anybody packing a pair of katars is someone you don't want to take lightly.

Knives

The knife is one of the oldest weapons made by man. The first knives were derived from stone hand axes flaked out of obsidian or flint. With short blades the limitations of stone as a medium for blade-making was lessened. They could be quite sharp, and the materials to make them were relatively plentiful. Swords themselves can be said to have grown out of the technology of the knife, being a process whereby people made longer and longer knives. At some point you had a sword, and the two weapons diverged over the centuries.

This section is dedicated to a specific set of implements designed to cut and pierce. By "knife" in the discussion which follows I mean a purpose-built knife designed to cut flesh, and perhaps secondarily to act as a utility tool. Kitchen knives, not meant to be weapons, are discussed in brief above. This still leaves a wide range of items to discuss. The term "knife" can be applied to a vast range of cutting tools both large and small. Some of them are folding knives meant to be carried in a pocket. Some of them are large cutting weapons meant to be used to attack an opponent or even split kindling. Some are hunting weapons meant to skin game. Some pierce, some slice and cut. Many do both.

Knives (and any other names you might use, like dagger, *saex*, dirk, stiletto, etc.) have been used as tools and weapons for thousands of years. They were used as specialized military weapons in the bronze age (3600-1200 BCE in the Middle East), and in all the ages that followed it. Daggers of various kinds filled in before metallurgy was advanced enough to make really useful swords, and they were often carried as close-combat weapons even when swords where available. Two famous examples of this are the Persian Immortals who fought as a royal guard for the Kings of Persia, and the Spartan hoplites who fought to the death against them at the Battle of Thermopylae in 480 BCE. Daggers were not the main weapons of either group—the Persians relied upon composite bows and stabbing spears, while the Spartans carried long spears to thrust over their wall of shields. But daggers were carried by both sides as close combat weapons, to be used when enemies were too close for the spear to be effective. While the Spartans considered their side arms to be swords, other Greeks remarked upon how short the blades of Spartan swords were. So, short even by Greek standards, these weapons can be understood to be wide-bladed daggers. The Spartans, always confident, meant to get very close to their enemies.

There are a vast number of different types of knives and daggers. Some of them were designed to have wide chopping blades, such as the Saxon saex (hence their name), while others were designed with pronounced, reinforced points like medieval stilettos. Often the blade form of a knife can tell you fairly precisely what task it was meant to perform. The stiletto, as you may have guessed, was designed to pierce deeply into vital organs. Late medieval daggers were often made to maximize the power of a thrust, a process driven by the growing durability of body armor. Weapons like the saex were designed for an age when most soldiers wore little armor, and so a broad cutting blade could slice and hack and still be lethal in a thrust. In the sixteenth century the Japanese produced daggers that were every bit as well made as their magnificent swords. Called a "tanto," a dagger of this type has a blade similar in geometry to those found on Japanese swords—they are single edged weapons with a thick spine at the back of the blade and a pronounced curved point. The spine provided rigidity to the blade, while the long cutting bevel and hard, sharp edge made it excellent at cutting and slicing. Such a dagger could stab even through armored targets and was just as deadly slashing at close range.

In the early nineteenth century a style of knife that is still famous was created in the southern US. It was and is known as the "Bowie" knife after its most famous user, James "Jim" Bowie, a plantation owner and adventurer who became famous for dying at the Alamo in 1831. Most Americans, if they connect Bowie with any historical event, probably link him with the failed defense of the Alamo fortress, which was overwhelmed by the Mexican army commanded by Santa Anna. But in 1831 Bowie was already famous, more or less, in particular for a violent altercation he took part in known as the Vidalia Sandbar Fight. This was a duel outside of Natchez, Mississippi, which took place in 1827 and included something like sixteen participants all together. Bowie was not meant to be one of the duelists—the two men who had called the duel each brought supporters, as was normal practice, and so on that particular day in 1827 both groups watched from the sidelines as the two combatants aimed their dueling pistols and fired. As the smoke cleared, it was obvious that both men had missed each other. Satisfied (or relieved, each to himself, that they didn't have fatal gunshot wounds) the two men approached each other and shook hands, which should have been the end of the duel. Honor had been satisfied. Unfortunately, the various supporters of the two were less than impressed, and as Bowie approached the relieved duelists all hell (as they say) broke loose. In the melee that developed between the two parties Bowie killed one opponent, who had just impaled Bowie on his sword cane, and cut part of the arm off another. In return he had a pistol broken over his head, suffered two or three stab wounds and absorbed three bullets. Bowie survived. The affair at the Vidalia Sandbar made Bowie's reputation as a badass, and he cemented it in subsequent years in knife fights and other bellicose undertakings. When he was overwhelmed at the Alamo he was so ill (the precise cause is unknown) that he was bedridden and unable to offer much resistance. It was probably lucky for the men who killed him. Had Bowie lived in another age he would have been an excellent friend to drag along through the zombie apocalypse.

The knife that made Bowie famous and still bears his name was originally a type of hunting knife (probably) commissioned by his brother, Rezin Bowie. Later, James had a larger knife made to his own specifications, the design seemingly influenced by Spanish and South American fighting knives. In its "mature" form, if such a term is possible to apply, the Bowie knife had a blade somewhere between nine and thirteen inches in length, with a clipped point. It was singled edged, save for the clip at the end of the blade which carried the edge along the back from the tip of the weapon for a few inches. The blade spines were quite thick, providing rigidity and mass which allowed the knife to cut, hack and stab with equal ferocity. A short cross-guard protected the hand and added to the effectiveness of the weapon in a fight. Sometimes there were reinforcements added to the back of the blade that extended from the hilt, a brass bar or bars that protected the back of the blade in the event it were used to parry an attack. Bowie knives were excellent close combat weapons, capable in the right hands even of beheading opponents in a fight. Moreover, the wicked appearance and size of these knives was often sufficient to halt attackers. No one wants to be gutted.

The many types of knives available offer a prospective survivor a multitude of choices. There are a number of factors to consider when choosing the knife or knives that you will be carrying. As always weight and portability is a factor to consider. The larger the knife the greater the weight, clearly, and some of the very largest such weapons are not inconsiderable. They can take up quite a bit of space, and in terms of porting any weapon or tool every ounce eventually adds up. It is only in the artificial world of video games where someone can get away with carrying an entire arsenal of tools and weapons without fatigue or encumbrance. In the real world everything you carry needs to be carefully considered and every addition of weight understood as a trade off. The use the blade will be put to is also something to keep in mind. Do you want a purpose-built anti-zombie weapon, meant to carve up and pierce through undead attackers? Do you want a back up weapon to supplement other items you might already be carrying? Do you want your knife to be capable as a utility blade as well as something that might work against zombies?

If the knife in question needs to be capable of serious combat duties, you should clearly choose the largest model you can effectively wield. In the modern US a whole variety of compact knives and firearms are available for consumers interested in concealing weapons for self defense. Thus you have both guns and knives designed to be as compact as possible while retaining at least close-range effectiveness. But the concept of 'concealability' is largely pointless in the middle of the zompocalypse. There are no authorities interested in punishing you for carrying a knife that is too big. Firearms need not be concealed. You can carry whatever you like, whatever you feel is most effective, since no laws have survived the collapse of society. The only scenario when a concealed weapon might be useful is one in which you envision yourself being captured by human enemies. If these hypothetical people don't look too carefully an extra hideout pistol or a knife might allow you to make your escape from death, slavery or cannibalism. The operative word is "might." so you can judge for yourself how paranoid you want to be. Other than this, if you want a fighting knife get the largest one you can wield. Modern proponents of knife fighting have developed a wide variety of popular how-to manuals and videos detailing the ins and outs of knife fighting. In my opinion many of these are largely useless for the average user. You can't learn how to "win" a knife fight in a few easy steps. Part of the problem is that most knives that are carried by so-called knife fighting experts are too small to be used as effective weapons in a fair fight. Large fixed bladed knives are usually constrained by legislation restricting their use. Thus you can see supposed knife fighters showing you how to essentially "duel" with something that is little more than a pocket knife. There is a reason Jim Bowie carried a knife with a foot-long blade. Combined with the guard it allowed the user to parry attacks, to use the knife as a defensive weapon. It was (just) long enough to stay out of range of an opponent's attacks. With anything much shorter than about 8" you're risking, or maybe even ensuring, that you get cut too. Knife fighting as portrayed in popular how-to videos is silly. Unarmored ancient warriors used shields. Later unarmored duelists carried parrying weapons in their off-hand or utilized swords that could be used as defensive weapons in their own right. The same goes for Japanese duelists, who fought with swords that could be used to deflect an opponent's weapons. A knife fight, as understood at the level of selling products over the internet, is a very stupid thing to get yourself into.

In any conceivable situation in the new undead-dominated world a bigger knife is a better knife, if you wish to use it for combat. Take a cue from Mr. Bowie and grab yourself something with reach and heft. The largest knives are very capable weapons, which can both cut and thrust to deadly effect. Against humans even small knives are absolutely lethal, which is the reason why police are generally instructed to shoot knife-wielding attackers if they close to within a certain distance. It makes sense if you consider what knives do to the human body. A gun, for example, kills by damaging the nervous system or causing massive and rapid blood loss. Guns are capable of carving fairly large holes in human targets. But the size of these often pales in comparison to what edged weapons are capable of. A bowie knife might carve a path three inches wide all the way through a victim's body. Swords are capable of even more severe trauma. If you can close with a human opponent, edged weapons are capable of inflicting unsurvivable wounds.

Pocket knives are not necessarily meant to be used as weapons, unless you mean as weapons of last resort. The ability to fold a knife in half allows it to be carried safely and without the need for a sheathe. It also takes up relatively little space. The problem with these knives at least as far as using them as weapons is that they are small and light. Even the largest folding knives are inferior to their fixed bladed cousins in terms of being used as weapons. Folding knives may be carried as backup weapons, but should be relegated to that duty or for use as tools, instead of being relied upon for self defense. This is not to say that the best of them are not well made –clearly they are—but given the lack of restrictions on concealed carry of personal weaponry in an apocalypse you really ought to try and find a longer and stouter weapon.

Medieval designs, the daggers and dirks that were meant as backup weapons for battlefield use are excellent choices, both against humans and undead enemies. Many reproductions of such implements are available, and they are not particular expensive. Usually these aren't really high quality items, most of them being made in China and India, but modern steel largely negates any shortcomings they might have. A foot of sharpened steel is effective even if it isn't exactly artwork. The same goes for the Japanese daggers, which were meant to be used in war as adjuncts to the longer swords and spears carried by the samurai. Practically any of these blades would serve you well against human or inhuman attackers, if nothing better is available.

As far as modern knife designs are concerned there are many makes and styles to choose from. From mass produced knives made by large companies like the KA-BAR combat knives (used by the USMC since the Second World War) to the most expensive hand-made custom bowie knives, an entire industry exists to fill your needs. Or at least it existed before zombies ate everyone, depending on when you're reading these pages. Anyway, the sky is the limit.

The very highest quality knives should last indefinitely. Whether these are fully handmade blades with fancy zone-tempering or produced from hi-tech modern steels with CNC machinery, high end knives will cut very well and last a long time. For all of these instruments it is highly necessary to have some means of sharpening the blade's edge when it is dulled through use. Sharpening by hand is not as easy as it looks—it would be a highly worthwhile endeavor for all survivors to master the techniques of sharpening knives, a skill that can be applied up the food-chain of bladed weapons to cover swords and axes as well. You don't necessarily need to have sophisticated sharpening paraphernalia, though good sharpening stones help a lot and do not take up much space. In a pinch you can sharpen your weapon on river rocks and use your belt as a sharpening strop to polish an edge. Knives, by their nature shorter and lighter than swords, lack the mass and momentum that can make a longer sword cut even with a reasonably dull edge. Knives need to be kept sharp. A few sharpening stones and ceramic rods are items to keep your eyes peeled for. In a world dominated by the undead, good scavenging skills will be rewarded.

Two of the more common mass produced modern combat knives are the KA-BAR and the Fairbairn-Sykes. The blade types of these two weapons are quite different from each other and tell the user quite a bit about how they were intended to be used. The KA-BAR, which is still made in large numbers for civilian and military use, has a wide cutting blade with a clip point. It can cut fairly well, and the point is capable of powerful thrusting attacks. The knives are fairly lightweight, durable, and have a leather grip which provides for good retention of the weapon in a fight. The medium length blade of the KA-BAR is adequate for use as a weapon, and the whole package is small and light enough to be easily carried on a belt or lashed to other equipment. The Fairbairn-Sykes knife is rather different and more specialized than the KA-BAR. Designed by William Ewart Fairbairn and Eric Anthony Sykes (based in part on Fairbairn's experiences in Shanghai prior to WWII, which included hundreds of street fights as part of the Shanghai Municipal Police), the Fairbairn-Sykes is essentially a stiletto with a diamond shaped double-edged blade. It is not incapable of cutting, but the design is really meant to emphasize thrusting attacks with the needle-like point. The length of the blade was actually determined by the amount of penetration deemed sufficient to stab through German overcoats of the kind worn during the Second World War. The originators of the knife codified their approach to knife fighting in a study that scientifically ranked the proper use of the blade and the areas of the human body that were most vulnerable to it. One of the key strikes with the Fairbairn-Sykes is a horizontal stabbing attack directed into the side of an enemy's neck, thereby severing the spinal column or slashing through the major arteries feeding the brain. Either way death was almost instant. Against zombies, the techniques of using this or any knife or dagger must be modified to take into consideration the peculiar nature of the opponent.

When using any knife against zombies, it must be remembered that you will have to get quite close to your undead target in order to attack. You will be in harm's way in a sense that is not as true for something like a sword or a shovel. Knives are close range weapons. In a knife fight against a human you need to take into consideration the blade of your enemy, which can strike and parry with great speed. Zombies, in contrast, are very slow. They have only one real weapon, their teeth, and so your defense will concentrate on keeping your soft bits away from the biting action of those teeth. At the same time your targets are relatively few with a knife in your hands. You have no choice but to aim for the brain, which as you know is protected by the skull. The largest cutting knives, like the bowies, may be capable of entirely beheading a zombie, which would neutralize the threat of the zombie even if it didn't destroy the brain. For most other knives, especially weapons like the Fairbairn-Sykes, the main attack should be a thrust aimed at piercing the skull at one of its weaker points. The frontal bone (*os frontis* in Latin) of the human skull is the most well defended point, so don't stab your zombie in the forehead unless you have no choice. Attacks directed against the sides or base of the skull are more likely to smash through to the brain, as are thrusts into the eye sockets, which are relatively thin and weak. Larger knives, especially those like the bowie knives which are equipped with crossguards to protect the hand, can be used to "fix" a zombie—that is, you thrust to impale the creature on your knife and then use the hilt in order to manipulate the zombie, perhaps to maneuver it towards an ally who can strike the death blow to the brain.

It is against single zombies where the knife begins to shine as a weapon—quick thrusting attacks are silent and allow you to quietly dispatch a lurking loner before he/she/it has the chance to draw other zombies to your position. Since zombies are not particularly fast or agile, overwhelming a single zombie with your knife should not be that difficult. Zombies do not recover well from being tripped or pushed over, and so you can take advantage of their lack of coordination to temporarily incapacitate them and strike to their brains before they can fully recover. Just remember to beware the teeth and you should have no problem.

Against pairs or small groups of zombies a good knife can be used to cripple individuals in order to fragment the pack into a more manageable threat. A key target in this scheme are the vulnerable tendons along the backs of the knees and the large muscle groups that make up the buttocks. Without the supporting tendons a zombie's legs will not function, even though they cannot feel pain. Similarly, inflicting enough damage to the gluteal muscles hampers movement. In this scenario the first zombie or zombies should be quickly slashed in order to slow its movement, allowing you to continue to retreat. Once enemy numbers have been thinned and the crippled zombies are crawling after you, the decision can be made to flee or go back and mop up.

Movies love to portray characters throwing knives, usually with lethal effect. While it is possible to inflict a dangerous (or even lethal) wound at close range by throwing a very large knife (like a bowie), the skill is difficult enough that it should be more or less ignored. Only the very heaviest knives are capable of doing much damage when thrown, at least in the hands of most users. Throwing a knife is a very difficult skill to master. Further, the only acceptable target for a human knife-thrower launching his weapons against zombies is the skull. Since the zombies in question are mostly certain to be approaching (hungrily), that means that you're trying to throw your knife at a moving target, a target that happens to be the hardest part of the human body, which is also handily sloped to deflect impact. Even if you manage by some miracle to destroy one zombie, it will come at the cost of you being disarmed. So don't throw your knives away. If you're down to only a knife and you need a missile weapon find a brick or a large rock. Keep the knife for hand to hand fighting.

The Machete

The machete is included here with the "real" weapons, as opposed to the discussion of improvised weapons that began this volume, because of all the tools commonly found in sheds or workshops the machete may be the closest in design to an actual weapon. Ostensibly an agricultural tool long used for a variety of chopping and cutting chores, machetes are common, durable, and lightweight. They also have a somewhat sinister history, having been put to use as a weapon in massacres and attacks on unarmed civilian populations. Machetes come in a variety of shapes and sizes, and are cheap to manufacture. Machetes are usually not constructed out of the highest quality steel, given that their primary task is to chop brush and branches in an agricultural setting. This means that they often can't be given a razor-sharp edge, and will be capable of holding only a utility edge (which still might be fairly sharp). A machete has a flexible blade, which allows it to absorb the impact of chopping resilient organic matter without permanently deforming. They are quite thin through the spine of the blade (nearly all of them are single edged), which is the primary difference between machetes and swords, which will have much thicker, heavier blades. Swords have considerably more mass than machetes do, in part because they were meant to be use against armor-wearing and shield-bearing opponents. Swords were designed to cut through relatively well protected targets, whereas a machete was designed to cut through saplings and sugar cane. Thankfully, zombies do not wear armor, nor do they know to dodge attacks—which allows you, the heroic machete wielding survivor, to concentrate your attacks on the skull and neck of your undead enemy.

Machetes are lightweight, which as you know is an important consideration when determining which items you'll be lugging around through the post-apocalyptic wasteland. Machetes were meant to be used by agricultural laborers performing long hours of manual labor. Their light weight allowed them to be used for long periods of time without completely exhausting the user. This is a significant difference from actual swords, which are heavy enough to tire the sword wielder, especially one that is out of practice or not in good physical condition to begin with. A decent machete can be a useful weapon in the zompocalypse, given that it combines a number of the features that are important in a hand weapon—reach, durability and light weight. You can easily pack one or more machetes on your person without really noticing it.

Though they were not meant to be used against humans (or zombies), machetes are nevertheless fairly effective weapons. A particularly nasty piece of evidence in support of this is the genocide in the African nation of Rwanda, which took place in a period of about one hundred days in 1994. In that span more than half a million members of the minority Tutsi population were slaughtered by their majority Hutu neighbors. Many or most of the victims of that slaughter succumbed to wounds inflicted by machete-bearing Hutus. A machete is capable of cutting into a human skull, even though the blade lacks the mass of medieval swords.

The inexpensive nature of the machete and its corresponding availability makes the machete one of the more common hand weapons you'll encounter as you wander through the detritus of civilization. You might have to look very closely to find a decent sword, but machetes are everywhere.

A machete can be used as a tool as well, and since you're going to be camping out (presumably), the multi-purpose nature of the machete should not be discounted. As with items like the crowbar or the haligan tool a machete can be put to a variety of uses. A sword can cut flesh and bone. It can't chop firewood, and will be damaged if put to this use. A machete can do many things, even though it doesn't cut or slash or pierce with the same effectiveness as a sword.

In battle the machete is somewhat more limited than swords, in that they really can't thrust very effectively. The blade of a machete is simply too thin and flexible to be much good in a thrust. This is exacerbated by their normally low-grade steel, which can only be made so sharp. Against a hungry zombie you're going to want to direct cutting attacks at the neck and the skull, to destroy or incapacitate the vestigial zombie nervous system. Thrusts should be avoided.

Machetes come in a variety of shapes and sizes. The most common are probably those that are patterned off of Latin American designs. Other styles exist, however, and many of these would be effective if pressed into service as weapons. The "panga" type machete has a blade that swells towards the tip, which increases the weight and momentum of the blade, resulting in more effective cutting strokes. A number of manufacturers make "kukhuri" style machetes, which have a forward canted blade of the same type as the Gurkha khukuris of Nepal. Like an actual kukhuri, such weapons are capable of effective cuts, though the much thinner blade of the machete is not going to be the cutting powerhouse that its heavier cousin is.

More exotically, some makers produce double-handed machetes, which would be even better adapted to lopping off zombified limbs and heads. They share the relative light weight and ease of carry of other machetes but allow two hands to be used if needed. I like to think of these as hand-and-a-half machetes—they can be used easily with one hand, but can make powerful two-handed cuts as well.

Machetes are so light and so ubiquitous that there is no excuse for not having at least a few of them around. If a safe base is found and potential storage is increased, every machete that can be found should be seized and stored away. As a bare minimum, if nothing better is at hand, every survivor could do a lot worse than starting off with a machete and a backup knife of some kind, even if that is only a kitchen knife. With a machete a lone survivor is capable of living long enough to procure better equipment. If you find a group of allies, machetes potentially become even more effective. Armed with machetes and some limited defensive equipment, a small group of savvy survivors should be capable of tackling fairly sizeable groups of zombies and emerging victorious.

The reduced cutting power of machetes is something of a trade off, with benefits and drawbacks not necessarily shared by actual swords. While their cutting performance will not equal that of medieval slashing swords, they are resilient and can be easily honed if the edge is damaged through use. They are meant to chop into fibrous materials, and the thin blades give them flexibility and the ability to be withdrawn quickly after a strike. Given the semi-squishy nature of zombies and the issues regarding weight restrictions, machetes are one of the key tools of the apocalypse. They are light weight enough to carry at all times, an important thing to consider in a changed world where danger can come suddenly from any direction.

Spears and Polearms

Through history spears and other pole weapons have been the primary arms of the infantryman. There are of course exceptions to this general rule, for example the Roman legionaries who were javelin-armed swordsmen, but more or less such a statement is accurate. There are a number of reasons why spears and polearms were so common. Firstly, they were cheap and relatively easy to make. Even a relatively poor-quality spear can still be an effective weapon. Metallurgy is more important for swords than it is for spears, and a crude sword might a liability in battle. Since a spear concentrates all its force on a small (and reinforced) point, the quality of the thing is somewhat less of a factor. Spears were extremely effective weapons despite their low cost, especially when used as part of an organized group of warriors. Their relative light weight meant that they were very fast weapons, difficult to block when used with skill. Their piercing blades, which were often two inches or more in width, could inflict terrible, fatal injuries. And they could do it efficiently. Impalement by a medieval spear point is going to cause more damage to a human target, generally, than most firearms are capable of inflicting. Ancient edged weapons are nothing to scoff at.

There are a number of modern makers who reproduce spearheads (often the shafts are not provided or sold separately due to shipping issues) for anyone wacky (or smart) enough to buy one. Some are sold for use as hunting implements, used notably in the southern US where some individuals utilize them to hunt the feral pigs that are a destructive introduced species in that part of the country.

The techniques for using a spear against the undead vary somewhat from how one would be used against human opponents. Against humans, the spear user will want to use the speed and reach of the spear to keep his opponent at a distance, making very sure to keep a sword or axe wielding enemy beyond the point of the spear. You'll want to keep your opponent at length if that opponent is undead, but the generally slow nature of zombies makes this less crucial than if you're trying to keep your limbs from being removed by a sword-stroke. Zombies are unimaginative (or non-imaginative?) fighters—their predilection for walking straight at their target works to the advantage of a spearman or spearwoman because he or she won't have to worry about the intended target dodging the blow. Just plant the point squarely in the center of the dead head and recover. Rinse and repeat, as it were.

The shaft of any pole weapon is a highly useful implement all on its own in the middle of a zombie melee. The shaft can be used to strike in the manner of a staff, in order to knock opponents off balance. Zombies can be tripped and thrust backward by the application of force and leverage. In close combat the shaft of a spear or polearm can be thrust sideways into a zombie's mouth in order to temporarily gag (and therefore disarm) it. The long shafts of pole weapons allow the user to stay out of harm's way while they inflict damage with the blade or point of their weapon. Even a stabbing spear can be used to slash, using the long shaft to build momentum.

The shaft of a spear has the benefit of being replaceable. If weight is a consideration it (and you know it is) it should be remembered that a spearhead is itself easily portable—the shaft can be made out of suitable wood with only a knife (and a little spare time). If the shaft breaks it can be replaced. The length of the shaft can be fine-tuned for the height of the individual user. Greek hoplite warriors of the fifth century BCE used spears with shafts that were seven or eight feet long. You (the savvy survivor) might not need such a long spear, and since customization is only a bit of whittling away this is an easy fix.

A particularly effective type of spear for really close combat is the "assegai," a short-handed spear which was the brainchild of Shaka Zulu, the nineteenth century Zulu chieftain who conquered an empire through a combination of innovative military tactics and sheer determination. The weapon of the Zulu warrior (at least after Shaka got done with him) was the assegai, a stabbing spear with a very short shaft. In use the assegai is not so very different from the Roman short sword, the gladius, that conquered a much earlier empire in the Mediterranean basin. The assegai is not meant to be thrown, though it might be if an emergency called for doing so. Instead, the assegai inflicts rapid, deep stabbing wounds on its victims. It was a deadly weapon that was only defeated by the modern rifles of the British army at the end of the nineteenth century.

Against zombies the assegai has a number of advantages to recommend it. It has decent reach, and is a quick weapon in the hands of skilled user. It is capable of slashing attacks in the manner of a sword, though these are less effective given the relative weight differences. Very effective in a thrust, an assegai should readily pierce through semi-decayed zombie opponents. It is easily carried into battle, and can be supplemented with other weapons. As the Zulu warriors used the assegai it was part of a weapons-system that included an ox-hide shield, which could be used to parry attacks. The spear would then snake out from behind the shield to inflict a lethal wound before being withdrawn again, ready for the next opponent. Against zombies some form of defensive tool held in the off-hand would increase the effectiveness of the Zulu thrusting spear, but even by itself it would be a powerful and effective weapon against the undead. Like other pole weapons, the shaft of the Zulu spear can be easily replaced if necessary. Indeed, a single blade could be used with a variety of shafts to adapt the weapon as needed to changing circumstances. A spear is truly a versatile weapon.

Polearms were certainly not limited to thrusting spears. Even in the bronze age the Chinese had a variety of different pole weapons, like the bronze dagger-axes that were carried by warriors who rode into battle on chariots. Both in Japan and Europe the medieval period was characterized by the growing importance and effectiveness of infantry soldiers armed with polearms. They were easy to learn to use, so lower class troops could be effective without having the life-long military experience that was restricted to aristocrats. Especially in groups polearms made common soldiers deadly. The medieval halberd (basically a combination of an axe and a spear on a long pole) could defeat mounted knights and hack through their heavy armor regardless of whether they fought afoot or on horseback. It could hook men off of their mounts, and deliver enormously powerful cutting blows. Charles the Bold, the last Duke of Burgundy, was literally split by a blow from a halberd in the hands of an angry Swiss soldier at the Battle of Nancy in 1477. In the late medieval period many aristocratic knights and lords perished under the heavy blades of halberds and other types of polearm.

Halberds and poleaxes are going to be relatively rare in the ranks of reproduction weapons. This is probably because they are not as sexy as swords, which is a more serious statement than it sounds. Swords are the romantic weapons of kings and knights, especially as understood in popular culture. The sword is a weapon that could be passed down through the generations. It was a means of displaying of wealth and power. It was status. A halberd or pole-axe is none of these things. It is a tool, just like a wood axe, though it is intended to split bodies and skulls and not firewood. Such weapons do not display status. They are not intended as heirlooms. They are only specialized tools for killing.

Against zombies the larger pole weapons are both very effective and somewhat overkill. Halberds are meant to split a human skull after you've already cut through the plate armor and padding protecting that skull. A spongy zombie doesn't need quite so much attention.

Bows and Crossbows

The bow is one of the oldest weapons used by man. Uncountable masses of people have been cut down by arrows in the course of human history. Their antiquity can be seen in the fact that Ötsi, the mummified Alpine ice-man who died in the late Chalkolithic (c. 3,300 BCE) was found with a stone arrowhead imbedded in his back. Over the course of human history many civilizations specialized in the bow as a weapon of war. The Egyptians were especially keen archers—it was Egyptian bowmen who slaughtered the invading Sea People at the Battle of the Delta (c. 1175 BCE). The Parthians who annihilated the Roman army commanded by Marcus Licinius Crassus at the Battle of Carrhae in 53 BCE were primarily horse-archers, as were the Huns who terrorized the Western Empire before it fell apart in the fifth century CE. The Mongols, who conquered the largest empire ever seen, were like the Parthians and the Huns in that their warriors were mostly speedy horse archers, who could weaken opponents with arrow fire before closing in for the kill. During the Hundred Years War (1337-1453 CE) the bow was a battle-winning weapon, in the form of the longbows utilized by English foot-archers. The bow was the most effective long-range weapon system for most of human history. It combined a high rate of fire with the ability to pierce armor, and specialized models could be fired from horseback as the steppe hordes ferociously demonstrated time and again. Bows were only eclipsed as battlefield weapons with the rise of effective muskets, a development of only the last few hundred years. The reason for the displacement wasn't so much that guns were inherently more effective as weapons—which they weren't, at least if you mean early matchlock muskets which were extremely slow to load and inaccurate even at close range—it was that guns were easier to use. The one weakness of bows is that they are difficult weapons to master, and they require physical strength and training on the part of their users. Guns were simple and cheap to manufacture, and they could be handed out to anyone. Guns made poorly trained soldiers effective on the battlefield, which meant that if a state had the money it could suddenly field a very large army. Bows needed specialized archers, ideally trained from birth. If you lost a bunch of your archers, it was difficult to find new ones. You couldn't just hand someone a bow and expect them to be effective with it overnight.

The primary problem with archery in the zombie apocalypse has everything to do with the question of physical ability and training. Most people in the modern world did not grow up learning to shoot a bow. If you did, good for you. I spent several years shooting compound bows as a boy, and so I understand the rudiments of archery, but many years have passed since then and now my experience is mostly a memory. If put to the test I could probably launch an arrow down range, but I'm hardly a master archer. If you've never shot a bow at all, you're going to have to spend some time practicing. On the up side of things, after all the electricity goes out you're going to have to find other things to do to occupy your time. There will be no internet in the zompocalypse. You might as well take up a useful hobby.

Bows can be effective weapons against the undead, if the hand wielding the bow has a certain amount of skill with one. That is potentially a very big "if." Don't engage a group of zombies with a bow unless you have backup weapons, a good escape route, or are absolutely certain of your skill as an archer. Bows have a relatively low rate of fire, unless the user is a master archer. Even then, there are only so many arrows you can loose. Another thing to keep in mind is that arrows are a lot bigger and bulkier than the cartridges for your 9mm Glock. The limitation of how many arrows a warrior could carry on his person (or his horse) limited the overall rate of fire of bows in combat. Launching arrows at the maximum rate of fire could exhaust an individual's ammunition supply in mere minutes. While arrows could be drawn out of the ground or taken from wounded or dead enemy soldiers, this was not a good way to resupply in the heat of battle. Sophisticated archers, like the Parthians who wiped out the Romans at Carrhae, used dedicated arrow-supply teams to rearm their archers as they used up each quiver of arrows. Thus there was little let-up for the Romans over the course of the battle and they were literally deluged with deadly projectiles for most of a day. You won't have minions to help you get more arrows, so keep in mind that ammunition for your bow is limited.

Arrows can be reused, if you have the ability to strip them from zombie corpses. If you're fighting a running battle you probably won't have time to stop and reclaim your spent arrows, so you'll have to be very careful with how you use your bow. Engaging a group of zombies armed only with a bow is a delicate business. Keep in mind as well that arrows can be damaged through use, with the shafts broken (or bent in the case of aluminum arrows) or the heads blunted or broken off. The notion that a bow gives you an endless supply of ammunition is a faulty one. On the other hand, if you have the requisite crafting skills, arrows can be manufactured from the environment. Stone or metal (or even glass) arrowheads can be fabricated without too much trouble, and as long as you can keep an arrow shaft straight and fletch it with something to stabilize it during flight, you've got another weapon.

The principle advantage of bows and crossbows against the undead is that they make very little noise when they are fired. Gunshots have a tendency to attract more zombies. Bows and crossbows do not. Used cautiously, an archer has the ability to silently eliminate zombies one by one, slowing thinning a group while remaining unheard and invisible. In the zombie apocalypse the archer is a scout and an assassin, not a front-line warrior. The low rate of fire and limited ammunition capacity relegates archery to ambushes and skirmishes, not full-scale battle. A battle-line, properly manned, should consist of warriors armed with guns and hand weapons, not bows.

Accuracy is obviously an issue with bows. Like guns they have only a small area on each zombie where their fire is effective. Arrows should be directed at the eye-sockets of your opponents, small targets that are attached to moving zombie bodies. Other than that, you'll have to pierce the skull to get to the brain behind it. This is not as hopeless as it sounds, of course. While the arrows and bolts fired by bows and crossbows cannot equal the sheer velocity of bullets, they have the advantage of focusing their energy on a much more acute point. Because of this arrows can use less energy to do fairly impressive damage to a target. Hunters routinely use bows to kill large game—an arrow fired from a powerful bow or crossbow is fully capable of going entirely through even a large animal. While you're probably not going to zip your arrows all the way through zombie skulls on a regular basis, as long as the arrow is on target you should get the job done most of the time. Again, the problem is the skill required to hit a small target under pressure. If you've got that, you're good to go.

Crossbows were heavily used both in the Far East (by the Chinese) and in the West by medieval European nations. They had some of the benefits of early muskets, in that they were easy to use. Bowmen were hard to find and difficult to train, but you could train a crossbowman with comparative ease. Crossbows stored the energy of their stocks and strings with a mechanical latch, meaning that the user could hold his fire until he needed to loose a bolt. Crossbows were useful in sieges, and the most powerful models could pierce even heavy armor. The problem with crossbows was that they were themselves not particularly cheap to manufacture, and so when simple guns came along everyone switched to the newer technology. Guns were both easy to use and cheap to make, which meant that the days of the crossbow were numbered.

Modern crossbows are technologically sophisticated, but they share many of the features of their medieval ancestors. The most powerful models use various kinds of mechanical aids to assist in the cocking of the mechanism. Crossbows with milder draw weights can be cocked by hand. Due to the need for cocking the bow and loading a bolt as separate motions, the rate of fire is lower for crossbows than for traditional bows. Thus they are even more relegated to ambush and assassination. If you're stuck with only a crossbow against an advancing band of corpses, you should start to look for an escape route.

Outside of the realm of actual combat, bows and crossbows are effective hunting weapons, and they give you the ability to feed yourself without alerting every zombie in a mile radius to your whereabouts. All manner of game can be taken with crossbows, though you should be prepared for your potential lunch to run. Since food supplies may be contaminated or looted, having the ability to hunt for game while remaining anonymous is an extremely valuable ability. While other survivors are turning to cannibalism or eating grass, you'll learn to subsist on venison or pork or small game. A much better choice than learning to like "the long pork," as it were.

A final word about bows and crossbows—they should be relatively easy to find. Since most survivors lack the requisite archery skills, bows and crossbows are less likely to have been looted by other desperate humans who got there (wherever that is) before you. If you can fire a bow, or if you have the space and time to familiarize yourself with one, then you are that much ahead of everybody else.

The Utility of Firearms

A good chunk of the pages that follow are dedicated to a discussion of firearms and how these weapons relate to warfare in a post-apocalyptic world dominated by zombies. I take it for granted that firearms are extremely important weapons for human survivors. In contrast to the recommendations of other authors, I argue that firearms are among the best weapons to use against zombies, despite the fact that they use finite ammunition resources that can and will run out. Guns are not necessary for survival, but they make combat against the undead easier, safer, and more effective. Guns allow survivors to do things that they could not if they were armed only with hand weapons or bows. They provide individual survivors and survivor communities with additional tactical options, and so they are important resources that should be sought out. Firearms and ammunition should be a prime target of scavenging, and these resources should be stockpiled at every opportunity. They are the one weapon system that allows a survivor to be equally effective against groups of zombies and human bandits. They are critically important.

Note that the access to firearms will vary wildly depending on what part of the world you happen to find yourself in when zombies precipitate societal collapse. Some parts of Europe have few guns due to legal restrictions on their ownership. An example of one such country is Britain, which has instituted severe gun control legislation in the past several decades. If the apocalypse hits when you're in one of these countries, your access to firearms and the ammunition to shoot from them will be extremely limited. This will impact your long-term survival, and you and other survivors will be forced to adopted alternative strategies in response.

Much of this book is written from the point of view of US citizens who will have access to firearms. Obviously if this is not your reality then you'll need to pay more attention to the sections of this book dealing with weaponry other than firearms. US citizens, as mentioned previously, exist in a sea of small arms and ammunition. With the onset of the apocalypse and the collapse of civilization, as more and more living humans are devoured or zombified the available weaponry will only increase, relative to the surviving population. If 99% of the human population is destroyed, Americans (at least) will have access to millions of extra firearms. In the near term, at least, there is no real fear of running out, as long as some basic scavenging behaviors are engaged.

Firearms are incredibly powerful weapons against zombies. They are also much safer to use than other weapons, because they allow the user to maintain a safe distance, even if this is very short, from the advancing undead. Pretty much any hand-held weapon can be used against zombies, and these can be surprisingly effective. It is true, as other authorities assert, that hand weapons do not run out of ammunition. But it is also true than in order to use these weapons you will nearly always be entering into the danger zone created by a zombie's arms and teeth. In order to use these weapons you must put yourself in danger. As such, there is always an inherent risk in engaging in hand to hand combat. More than this, hand weapons are limited in that the number of zombies that can be destroyed quickly is limited. The "rate of fire," if you will, of hand weapons is limited by the ability of the weapon to destroy the zombie brain and/or spinal cord, and recover to do so again. As you tire, this "rate of fire" will inevitably degrade. Go into your back yard and swing a shovel or other implement, and time yourself. Do this for two or three minutes and you'll notice that you tire quickly. From this point of view, it is not actually correct to say that hand weapons have unlimited ammunition. They are quite limited, in practice, by your ability to swing with deadly force.

You are unlikely to kill as many zombies in a short space of time with a hand weapon as you are with a firearm, even if you have only moderate skill with guns. While the actual target area on a zombie is small, it is also a target area that moves in one direction (forward, towards you) and does so fairly slowly. With some minimal practice pretty much anyone can cut down a group of zombies, and they can do so without growing tired. Guns alone grant this advantage against the undead. Hand weapons are very important weapons, and are useful in ways that guns are not. But nothing allows people (even relatively unskilled people) to quickly engage multiple opponents like a gun.

Guns are really the only weapons that allow survivors to engage in a linear battle against the undead. Individual zombies, or even small groups, can be engaged with hand weapons depending on the skill level and physical fitness of the survivor in question. But large groups cannot be engaged in the same way. If you are lucky enough to be in the unlikely position of belonging to a large group of highly skilled and uniformly trained survivors, then hand to hand combat is viable. Well trained human warriors with shields and/or some form of body protection should be able to form a phalanx that would be quite effective against zombie bands. Hand weapons would suffice in this situation. But as I say, this scenario is most unlikely once the zombie apocalypse progresses to its mature form. When most humans are dead you won't be able to mass the numbers needed to pull off an old-fashioned infantry phalanx. You won't have the luxury of ensuring that each member is equally trained, equally healthy, and equally prepared psychologically. So hand weapons must in almost every case be limited to skirmishes and ambushes. Battle, which will be discussed in greater detail below, is the province of firearms. What follows is a wide-ranging discussion of firearms and ammunition, and how these technologies apply to the conditions of the zompocalypse.

Cartridge and Caliber

Guns need ammunition (obviously) or they won't do you any good. Well they could be used as clubs, I suppose, but as noted previously there are a lot of things that could be used as clubs. You should stick with a more appropriate club if you need to club something, so you'll need ammunition for your appropriate anti-zombie gun(s). There are a bewildering variety of guns which shoot an equally bewildering range of ammunition. The US firearms industry is something on the order of about three hundred companies raking in billions of dollars in yearly profits. The variety part is something to consider, in a number of ways.

One concerns the access to ammunition you're going to have in the zompocalypse. With no electricity and all the workers eaten (or eating as may be the case) ammunition factories will not be churning out their regular quota of bullets and shells. No new ammunition will be produced unless it's made by individuals set up for manual home-based reloading. That means the gun caliber you end up using needs to be carefully chosen, if there is a choice to be made. Not all ammunition is created equally, in several meanings of that phrase. You're going to have a lot easier time finding a box of, say, shells for a twelve-gauge shotgun than you are the appropriate rounds for a revolver chambered in .475

Linebaugh. The most common calibers are ones you should be focusing on. This is a function, in part, of the commercial society that will have been snuffed by the rise of the zombies. The most popular calibers got purchased more often, which meant that more of them were made, which translated into more being made and prices going down and the caliber getting more popular in a capitalist feedback loop. The most common calibers are going to chamber in the most common firearms, so you're more likely to discover a twelve-gauge shotgun for the twelve gauge shells than you are the powerful handgun from the example above. Still, firearm choice needs to take into account the ammunition that you'll be firing. In no particular order you should keep your eyes peeled for the following types of ammunition: 1) 12 and 20 gauge shot shells 2) 9mm Luger 3) .45 ACP 4) .38 Special 5) .357 Magnum 6) .45 colt 7) .44 Magnum 8) .44 Special 9) 5.56mm Nato 10) .223 Remington 11) 7.62 x39mm 12) and last but certainly not least, .22 Long Rifle. Guns chambering these cartridges are going to be the most common firearms you encounter, and you'll find the ammunition for them to be the most plentiful of your many possible choices. Some of the list above is predicated on the notion that the US Government is a massive producer of ammunition in its own right, with government ammunition factories pumping out billions of rounds a year in military calibers. Some of these are for .50 caliber and 20mm machineguns and cannons that won't have much utility to the average zompocalypse survivor. But there are still great quantities of highly useful 9mm and 5.56mm rounds made that will be extremely useful when the dead rise.

If you have the ability to be picky, the above list can be pared down into more or less desirable choices. If you have ever paid attention to gun people talking about guns among themselves, you've noticed that many calibers have special fans who defend the characteristics of their particular caliber as being the best one for a variety of situations, whether it's hunting or self-defense or target shooting. The discussion of which pistol/revolver caliber is best for self-defense is particularly notable for the fervor with which the fans of this or that caliber seek to forward their opinions. Their discussions are only partially useful for the discussion of a zombie-related collapse of society.

Essentially, the long and drawn out argument about which type of gun and which caliber cartridge is best for self defense can be divided into two basic camps: those who favor bigger slower bullets and those who think smaller faster ones are better. The two sides are divided along the lines of what types of damage are best to quickly incapacitate a human aggressor. The big & slow faction argues that larger bullets hit harder and somehow "shock" the hypothetical assailant. Large-caliber bullets like the common .45 ACP thump into a human body and make a larger hole than smaller calibers. They are also made in modern hollow point varieties that will expand as they wound even at lower velocities. Such bullets might end their path into a human body having mushroomed out to nearly twice their original size. Having a 3/4" hole punched in you is obviously a bad thing, and so the pro-big-bullet people like guns that fire big bullets like the .45 ACP and the .45 Colt that was its inspiration. The fast bullet clan argues back that velocity ensures maximum penetration and only penetration counts when trying to incapacitate an attacker. Smaller bullets going fast poke smaller holes in their targets, but they do tend to poke a longer hole than the big fatties. The queen of the fast-is-better types has to be the now-venerable .357 magnum. Which is best? Good question.

There is some evidence to suggest that the fast bullet guys are right. An FBI study performed in the late 1980s found that much of the body's response to being shot is actually psychological and socially conditioned. That means that most people who get shot behave as they've been unconsciously trained to behave by society: they fall down. Scientifically speaking, the only thing that can cause immediate incapacitation from a gunshot wound (as the FBI paper argued) is destruction/disruption of the central nervous system or unconsciousness and death brought about by loss of blood. The problem with that is that even with destruction of the heart the brain still has enough oxygen to function for 10 or 15 seconds, which may be a long time in the middle of a gunfight. Yet most people who get shot drop. The FBI argued heavily against the notion of "knockdown power" that big-bullet people (and Hollywood movies) embrace. With small arms, especially handguns, there simply isn't enough kinetic energy imparted to a bullet to knock a human down. The size disparity is simply too great. What the FBI's argument supports is that to some extent the size of the bullet is irrelevant (in terms of handgun rounds). By the line of reasoning forwarded in the study, penetration is the most important thing a bullet can do, in that only by carving a path through a human body and severing major arteries can it reliably stop an aggressive human foe. If you're talking about human attackers (and those will definitely exist after the collapse of civilization) the above arguments are worth following. If the primary enemies are zombies that will only be destroyed with a shot to the brain, we're talking about a different "animal" entirely.

If zombies are our chief foe (and they are, if they've already eaten most of civilization) then a different set of parameters comes into play. One is that penetration is a primary concern. Another is related to the portability of ammunition. For the first the discussion seems fairly obvious—there are at most about two good targets for a survivor (or survivors) attempting to gunfight their way out of a zombie ambush, these being the brain directly through the skull or the spinal cord down the back and base of the neck. Shoot that, and your zombie will drop. Shoot something else, and he or she (it?) will continue to pursue lunch. Which may be you. So accuracy is of crucial importance. But power is less a factor. The fact is that all of the calibers listed above will be more than adequate to penetrate sufficiently given the right conditions. Bullets lose energy the farther they travel, and so range is theoretically a factor. What negates this is that your targets are small, so you'll be shooting at short ranges for the most part. At close range all guns are "gun enough" for zombies. In fact, most of the above are actually overkill, a waste of metal and energy for the purposes of destroying a reanimated corpse.

When considering which gun and the associated ammunition you'll be toting around, a key consideration should be the weight and bulk of both items. Twelve gauge shotguns are effective. But they are heavy, as is their ammunition, which is also physically bulky. There are only so many shotgun shells the average person can lug around, and since flight is going to be in many cases preferable to fight, weight and bulk are important. To remain spry and avoid grisly chewing you're going to want to be quick. Think ninja rather than samurai. One of the most underrated choices (in my opinion but also the opinion of many others who are knowledgeable about such matters) is the .22 Long Rifle and the many (many) handguns and rifles chambered for that cartridge. Some history is appropriate.

The .22 Long Rifle is a rimfire cartridge of great antiquity (well, antiquity as far as cartridge firearms are concerned). The technology of metallic cartridges was developed in the mid-nineteenth century around the time of the American

Civil War. It was during the course of that conflict that the first really practical weapons were developed that fed metallic cartridges. The technology was used sparingly during the war, in part due to problems related to the expenditure of ammunition. Soldiers in combat like to shoot (it makes you feel better) and if they can shoot faster they do so. The logistics of the time made it a serious factor—the top brass of the day didn't want their soldiers blowing through reams of expensive ammunition for nothing, and so paper cartridges and muzzle loading rifles remained. Anyway, cartridges arrived by midcentury.

There were some more oddball designs for the first metal cartridges. One was the "pin fire" system, in which a small metal pin protruded at a ninety degree angle from the base of the cartridge. This pin was struck by a falling hammer when the trigger was pulled, and the pin activated the round's charge and spat the bullet down the barrel. Rimfire was a more effective technology that eclipsed things like pin fire, and rimfire cartridges have been in production ever since. With rimfire technology the inside of the shell's base contains an explosive charge that is ignited when a firing pin strikes the cartridge forcefully. There is no primer in the sense of a center-fire cartridge which uses a separate primer recessed into the base of the cartridge. Rimfire was revolutionary for its day and the fact that it has continued in production ever since is testimony to its effectiveness. Generally rimfire is less reliable (in terms of ignition) than are centerfire cartridges, but modern ammunition (especially more expensive stuff) can be trusted. There are pressure limits to a rimfire cartridge—the shell casing has to be thin enough to fire when struck, and so you can't make the case thick enough to handle really powerful charges—but for what they are they are quite effective.

I advocate the use of the .22 Long Rifle (and the many firearms that chamber it) for a number of reasons. One is that it is very common. Ammunition for a .22LR handgun or rifle can be found throughout the US (and also in many countries that restrict guns and gun ownership). In the southern US (especially) it is everywhere. You can find it in hardware stores. In gas stations. At Walmart (also everywhere in the south). In people's houses. We're surrounded by a sea of tiny .22 caliber shells, people.

In conjunction with the ubiquitous nature of the rounds, the guns that fire them are extremely common. Many people learn how to shoot using .22 rifles. The low pressure of .22 Long Rifle means that with proper maintenance the weapons will last indefinitely. Browning automatic .22 rifles from the early part of the twentieth century are still around, and still plinking cans, dirt clods, paper targets and small game. Guns that fire .22 Long Rifle are legion. Another dimension to my advocacy stems from the small size and weight of the cartridges themselves. A box of 500 .22 shells only weighs about 4.5 pounds. They are extremely inexpensive, maybe one tenth the price per round of even relatively low-priced ammunition like the

5.56mm rounds fired by US military rifles. While everything is essentially free (if scavenged) during the zompocalypse, the capitalist cost effectiveness of the .22 means that they're everywhere and in great numbers. Thousands and thousands of rounds are packed in small spaces waiting to help save your life. The tiny size of each cartridge means that you can amass more rounds than you can conceivably need (if you're preparing in anticipation of the apocalypse, the inexpensive .22LR is not something to scoff at). Large amounts of ammunition are easily portable. In combat in Vietnam during the late 1960s my Dad carried an M2 carbine, a small .30 caliber rifle based on a design from the Second World War. He preferred the gun over the then-standard M14 because the ammunition was small and lightweight. He could (and did) carry far more ammo than was regulation (see above about soldiers liking to shoot). The same thing is basically good advice for combat involving zombies—the more bullets you have the better, because you will be outnumbered. You can pack a 12-gauge shotgun and 30 or 40 rounds of ammunition, or you can carry a .22 and hundreds of shells. Does that help make my case?

Hollywood incarnations of the zombie movie tend to be in love with what are in some ways some of the two worst weapons for a zombie-fueled collapse of society—the chainsaw, discussed above, and the 12-gauge shotgun. The shotgun is not worthless, of course, but it has a number of drawbacks that make it less than ideal. More to the point, since we're discussing ammunition, is the fact that 12-gauge shells are big and heavy. The shotgun itself recoils heavily (get used to bruises, if you bruise easily) and a lot of the power of the round is wasted on a zombie. Against human aggressors a 12-gauge shotgun is a fantastic weapon, perhaps the deadliest thing you can carry at close range. But only a head shot counts on a zombie. That means most of the buckshot will miss your target, hitting 1) nothing, which is useless 2) your zombie or another zombie in the limbs or torso, also useless 3) your friends, which is much worse than useless. Shotgun slugs are clearly effective, but they're big, heavy and a waste of energy.

The humble .22 Long Rifle will come to be a valued friend in the event of any apocalypse, not just one precipitated by the undead. It can be used to hunt small game very effectively, and in a survival situation (it is illegal to use on larger game animals in the US) when there are no rules you'll be hunting lots of things with your trusty .22. It is the perfect weapon for use against zombies, in part because the round has so little recoil that it can be fired quickly and with great accuracy at close range. The small 38 or 40 grain bullets travel somewhere between 1000 and 1600 feet per second (depending on the ammunition and the length of the weapon's barrel) which means it can easily penetrate a human skull at close range. If the bullet deflects, low recoil means you can try again in a split second. Lots of ammo means you'll have extra to encourage you to make the follow up shots.

With the right weapon .22 Long Rifle is even a good choice against dangerous human enemies. This statement is controversial—nobody (well, some limited use is made of them, but basically nobody) uses the .22 Long Rifle as a military round. Civilian self defense consensus in the US seems to be that it should be used in a self defense scenario only in the absolute last resort. If nothing else is available, goes the argument. My unscientific guess is that many of the people making that argument are probably the big-bullet types who think you can only be considered armed if you've got a .45 caliber Colt 1911. The thing is, .22 Long Rifle will penetrate about a foot through soft tissue, which is more than sufficient to kill. The bullets are small, but there is no medical care, a fact which people will be very aware of in a zombie or any other type of apocalyptic societal collapse. You're back, for all intents and purposes, in the Middle Ages as far as medicine is concerned. If your (say) bandit enemy doesn't go down after the first shot, keep going. You'll already be good at headshots, having practiced on all the zombies between point A and point B.

A final note about the .22 Long Rifle is in regards to suppressing it. Not banning it, if you're unfamiliar—what I mean is "silencing" it in the jargon of popular culture which tends to call suppressors by the inaccurate term "silencer." Suppressors are legal to own in most US states at the current time, though you need special permission to buy one and they are fairly expensive. Essentially a suppressor is a tube with a complex pathway of hollows for hot expanding gas to get lost in. In the miniature maze at the end of the barrel the gas that drives the bullet slows down as it leaves the muzzle, reducing the noise made by firing. If the ammunition in question is also flying slower than the speed of sound (it's subsonic, baby) then the report of the rifle or handgun is even quieter. With the right ammunition a .22 caliber firearm can be made as quiet as a pellet rifle. That means that zombies won't be attracted from miles away. The guy that bought the shotgun is going to go down in a (short lived) blaze of glory as he alerts all the hungry zombies in his immediate area at the very moment he spends his last shell. While he's being tenderized besides an empty twelve gauge you will be quietly eradicating your local herd of shamblers. Suppressors made for .22 caliber guns are the cheapest, most common and most effective of their kind. In a pinch you can also make them (illegal, but again with that no-law thingy). Against human opponents a .22 caliber rifle with a suppressor is a deadly weapon in a land with no medical care. Grumpy post-apocalyptic marauders are going to have a hard time telling where the bullets are coming from, given that the impact of the bullet is about as loud as the report of the weapon. Note that at close range your opponent may have enough oomph left to do you in before he or she expires from your .22 slugs. At extremely close range it may be a good idea to have a backup weapon firing a larger diameter round. Thus the other cartridges on the list above are far from useless, as we shall see.

The most common of the calibers mentioned previously are probably the .38 Special, the 9mm Luger, the .45 ACP and the 5.56mm NATO military cartridge. The first three are pistol rounds, all of them quite old, dating from the first decade or so of the twentieth century. They chamber in a wide range of commonly available pistols and rifles that are all tested and reliable weapons. All three are relatively low pressure cartridges, which means they won't strain the pistol or revolver. That in turn means that even old guns (if kept in reasonable condition) will still be serviceable. The 5.56mm is the standard round used by the US armed forces and our allies in NATO. It is common because US federal arms suppliers pump out vast quantities of this round to maintain military stockpiles. The popularity of M4 style automatic rifles among the civilian population (the M4 is the great-grandchild of the Vietnam era M16) and the large number of custom rifles and aftermarket parts means that both the gun and the rounds it chambers are common. Note also that overrun Army/Marine/National Guard positions will probably have a number of these (and other) weapons lying around. The 5.56mm can be suppressed, though it won't be as quiet as the much smaller .22 Long Rifle. All of these cartridges are lethal to the human body. At point blank range you're probably better off trusting in a larger caliber weapon than a .22, and so all of these rounds and the weapons that go with them are good choices.

Modern bullet technology has greatly magnified the effectiveness of handguns for civilian self-defense (armies are constrained by the Geneva Convention of 1949 to use only "ball" ammunition, that is, solid round-nose bullets). Civilian and law enforcement circles are free to use modern hollow-point expanding bullets that can both penetrate deeply and mushroom in a wound channel, cutting a much larger path than a typical solid projectile. Against human opponents (and these will be present and potentially very dangerous, as they will be armed with guns and other weapons just like you) carrying a revolver or pistol in one of the common calibers above is a very good idea. They are all more than effective enough to blast through a zombie skull as well, so you get more bang for your buck, so to speak.

Cap and Ball

The first really effective repeating firearms were developed in the middle of the nineteenth century by the American firearms pioneer, Samuel Colt. In the 1830s Colt created the Patterson revolver, which used a revolving cylinder to fire in succession a series of shots. While these weapons seem archaic from our modern perspective they were revolutionary for the day. A Colt revolver magnified the firepower available to the individual by several times over. Whereas before a soldier or armed civilian was limited to only a shot or two (for those carrying a brace of pistols) in the post-Colt era someone could fire off five or six shots per revolver without reloading. In certain respects these inventions were the assault weapons of their day, before the introduction of magazine fed rifles during by the time of the American Civil War. Colt refined his designs over the years, pioneering the large Walker and Dragoon model revolvers that were meant mostly as military weapons. By the Civil War Colt and his competitors (Remington and Smith & Wesson chief among them) had streamlined the design of the revolver into a reliable weapon that could be worn on a belt holster and conveniently carried as a sidearm. All of these early revolvers used the technology of the percussion cap, just as the military rifles of the day did. With this technology each shot needed to be loaded individually from the front of each chamber in a revolver cylinder (or from the muzzle with shotguns and rifles). A powder charge was measured into each of five or six chambers and followed by a soft lead ball or conical bullet. In revolvers a loading lever acted as a ramrod to force the ball or bullet tightly into the chamber. Once this was done the user would prime each cylinder with a small metal percussion cap, a tiny metal cup that contained the explosive charge that would ignite the main charge in each chamber and propel the projectile out of the weapon's muzzle. The caps were burst by the falling of a manually cocked hammer, which crushed them upon small cylindrical "nipples" at the back of each chamber. Once empty a revolver (or rifle) using such a system needed to be reloaded again by the same laborious process. Revolvers were so slow to load that they could generally not be reloaded in the middle of combat, leading soldiers (especially) to carry more than one pistol in order to ensure that they could continue to defend themselves. The propellant used was black powder, a slow-burning gunpowder that tended to foul the weapons with burnt powder residue. Muskets and rifles could be fired several dozen times at most before they began to grow so encrusted with fouling that they would no longer function. Revolvers were even more vulnerable to this, given their comparative mechanical sophistication. Despite this they were effective and deadly weapons, especially for their time. The soft lead balls and bullets expanded upon impact, creating gruesome injuries that commonly resulted in fatal infection in the cases where they did not kill outright.

It might seem silly to include a section on archaic nineteenth century firearms and firearm technology, but in the event of an undead apocalypse the reader may find himself resorting to whatever is at hand, and that may be a percussion firearm. I do not mean (if you're wondering) actual nineteenth century guns, which are in general antiques that are both valuable and too dangerous to fire. I mean reproductions of such weapons, which are actually more common that you might suppose. Quite a few manufacturers (such as the Italian gun makers like Pietta, or the company founded by Aldo Uberti) produce copies of nineteenth century percussion firearms. Enthusiasts of these old-fashioned weapons hunt with them and use them in historical re-enactments and target shooting. In general they are inexpensive to own and shoot, although they are labor-intensive in terms of the cleaning and care of the weapons due to the nature of black powder. Just as in the nineteenth century percussion firearms are slow to load, and cannot be recharged during combat with zombies any more than they can be in the midst of a gunfight with other humans. They are for all intents and purposes a one-off weapon, to be used until empty. Once the hammer goes "click" instead of "bang" another weapon must be obtained. Percussion firearms are generally heavy and would make acceptable bludgeons in a pinch, capable of cracking a human skull. Other than this, the option once you're empty is flight.

The advantage of percussion rifles and pistols is largely in terms of the fact that most people probably won't loot the associated ammunition or the guns themselves. They'll take the more obvious things like M4 rifles and shotguns and so on, and leave the antiquated stuff behind. This means that you may find yourself in possession of a number of archaic firearms and a pile of powder and lead bullets that other survivors have passed over in favor of other weapons.

Percussion firearms should never be anyone's first choice, obviously, in the constant hunt for a means of defense in the midst of a world-eating plague of zombies. But if your other option is a penknife or a chainsaw or something else equally impractical, then a decent reproduction Colt or Remington revolver might end up being a life-saver. Knowing how to load and manipulate percussion firearms might keep you alive long enough to get access to better equipment. They might be primitive from our modern perspective, but percussion technology inflicted considerable carnage up to and past the time of the American Civil War.

Even as the cartridge era made percussion obsolete, many people continued to make good use of existing percussion firearms into the 1870s and 80s. One especially notable figure to do so was James Butler "Wild Bill" Hickock, famous as a gunfighter, lawman and dime-novel celebrity. Murdered (he was shot from behind) in 1876 in Deadwood South Dakota, Hickock died in a time when cartridge firearms, especially those produced by the Colt and Winchester companies, were quite prolific. Yet he still carried two 1851 Colt Navy revolvers, six-shot .36 caliber weapons that operated with the percussion system.

Reproduction percussion rifles and pistols use slow-burning black powder, and they tend to fire their soft lead projectiles at lower velocities than most modern firearms. This is not especially important against undead enemies. All of the reproduction nineteenth century arms should be more than adequate for cutting through a skull into the zombified brain behind it. The most common percussion pistols are the so-called Army and Navy revolvers, chambered in .44 and .36 caliber respectively. Despite their low velocity these guns achieve impressive accuracy and the soft lead bullets and round balls expand readily. They won't pierce body armor (silk and cotton bullet resistant vests did exist but were rarely used), but zombies don't come in an armored variety. Against human opponents (raiders or bandits, say) it should be remembered that while you only have a few shots, they are sufficient to get the job done, provided you do your part. A great many people were killed by soft lead bullets fired with black powder. In terms of a zombie apocalypse it should also be remembered that medical aid will be sparse to non-existent, which means that someone shot with a .36 caliber round ball will for all intents and purposes relive one of the grim aspects of nineteenth century combat. Without medical attention, even a flesh wound can be fatal. If the bullet strikes a bone it will most likely shatter it—there is a reason why there were so many amputations performed during the course of the Civil War. The soft conical bullets (.577 and .58 caliber in the standard rifles) expanded on contact and were more than heavy enough to pulverize bone. In such a situation, without antibiotics and modern sanitary medical care the end result was death through gangrene, if the victim survived shock and blood loss.

The ammunition for percussion pistols and rifles comes in several separate containers. In the nineteenth century there were pre-made paper cartridges that simplified the loading process. These were actually a key component of military rifles and fire drill during the Civil War, with loose ammunition being much slower to utilize. Pistols could be loaded with pre-made cartridges as well, which were constructed with specially treated paper and loaded into the chambers whole. The drawback to these paper cartridges is that they were fragile and could break apart, leaving the user with a useless powder residue and a bullet. Their ignition was also not as reliable as the later metal cartridges that supplanted them.

If you load yourself up with a brace of Colt or Remington revolvers (or even more, if you want to copy the Civil War guerilla fighters who could carry as many as six or eight revolvers distributed about their persons and in saddle holsters) you won't have to worry about paper cartridges because all of the ammunition you'll encounter will be loose powder and balls/bullets. There are three essential components that you'll need, and a number of possible supplemental items. First you have to have black powder, or a black powder substitute (sold under various names, they create equivalent pressure to black powder and usually burn cleaner). This is the main propellant charge that with fire your ball or bullet. Powder is sold in bulk containers, both flat metallic tins and in larger plastic jugs. Powder needs to be handled carefully—keep flame and anything that could spark well away from your powder, or you'll (literally) go up in smoke. On the plus side, black powder is fairly lightweight and will provide you with plenty of potential shots. You don't need to grab twenty pounds of it. You'll need projectiles, of course, and these come packaged in square plastic containers. Both round balls and conical bullets are available. These will be much heavier than the powder you need—which should be obvious, since they're made of solid lead. Round balls may be a more attractive option, because they allow you more shots per pound than the heavier bullets. There's no reason to waste metal, since only a headshot counts anyway.

You are likely to find bullet molds as well, which look like miniature metal presses with two handles. If you think you'll be relying on your revolver for a while, you might think about grabbing the press. With this item you'll be able to make your own bullets as long as you can locate some lead—think of lead wheel weights on all the abandoned cars you'll encounter and you get the idea. Molten lead is poured into the mold, allowed to briefly cool, and when the press is popped open a formed bullet or ball drops out. Once you cut away the extra material from where the lead was poured you have yourself your very own lead ball (or bullet). Note that lead fumes are bad for you and you should take care to avoid breathing them. Since you'll be in the midst of societal collapse with cannibalistic walking corpses and crazed bandits, lead fumes might not be high on your priority list, but still, safety first. This simple bit of technology will allow you to make your own bullets if you run low on the factory made variety. It's worth considering, at least.

The third important component of your percussion ammo reserve are the all-important percussion caps that will set off your powder. These come in small round tins (usually in quantities of 100 per tin). Percussion caps are lightweight and plentiful—the average person could easily carry hundreds or thousands of them. Note that they come in different sizes, and so you'll want to familiarize yourself with your specific firearm enough know which size cap fits best on your revolver (I assume that most survivors would choose a revolver over the heavy single-shot percussion rifles that are available, since they must be loaded with loose ammunition after each shot).

There are a number of greases and greased patches or wads that modern black powder shooters use to seal the ends of their revolver cylinders. Once the charges are loaded and the balls or bullets are seated each chamber mouth is covered over or greased shut (the patches actually separate the powder from the bullet or ball, but the purpose is the same). At this point the weapons can be capped and fired or kept loaded for immediate use. With the chambers sealed (whether this is grease or with a patch) the gun is assumed safe from a type of malfunction known as a "chain fire," where firing one chamber ignites neighboring chambers. A chain fire is clearly a bad thing—you may end up losing parts of your hand if such a thing should occur. For this reason modern safety-conscious shooters seal their chambers and assure the well-being of their various digits. Chain-fires are rare, however, and most of them seem to be brought about through the rear of the cylinder, where the caps and percussion nipples are. In the event of a world-wide zombie apocalypse the chance of a chain-fire might be well down on your list of potential dangers. It is something to keep in mind. Malfunctions in general are to be expected when using percussion weapons. They were and are more reliable than the earlier flintlock weapons, but they are not modern firearms using metallic rimfire or centerfire cartriges. When using a percussion revolver (or rifle or shotgun) you will experience episodes where the gun doesn't do what you want it to do. Misfires are probably the most common issue—the percussion cap will fail to ignite your powder charge. You'll need to get another cap and try to ignite the chamber again. Another type of problem is known as a hang fire, where the powder charge is slow to ignite. Don't—safety first, remember?—look down the barrel to see what's going on. Percussion revolvers may also jam (in my experience the Colt-style reproductions are more prone to this than others) when a burst percussion cap falls down to interrupt the cylinder mechanism. If you rely on one of these weapons to protect your soft bits from nibbling zombies you should remember to stay on your toes, so to speak. The order of priorities should be 1) Next chamber! Die!, 2) Club it! Die!, 3) I'm getting out of here! So long, guys!

Revolvers

A revolver is a handgun which utilizes a revolving cylinder to hold a number a rimfire or centerfire cartridges. As the action of the weapon is worked the cylinder rotates to bring a fresh cartridge into battery. A revolver can be fired as long as an unfired round remains in the cylinder. Traditionally revolvers held five or six cartridges, but depending on the caliber and the weapon there are revolvers available that will hold up to ten rounds in a full cylinder. The revolver, if we're going to get technical, is a type of handgun. It is not a pistol, which refers instead to those handguns whose operation is semi-automatic and fed via a spring-loaded magazine.

As you know from the prior discussion of cap-and-ball technology revolvers were the first effective and mass-produced repeating firearms. Up until the late 1860s they were reliant upon the percussion cap, which is effective but not always reliable. By the early 1870s the technology of bored-through cylinders combined with self-contained metallic cartridges to produce the first handguns that modern people would be automatically familiar with. The most prevalent of these revolvers were the .44 and .45 caliber revolvers made by the company started by Samuel Colt. Colt's revolvers were adopted as the official

US Army sidearm and used as such for the last decades of the nineteenth century. They (and their competitors, made by Remington and Smith & Wesson, among others) were enormously popular with civilians and law enforcement officers well into the twentieth century.

These early cartridge revolvers all operated via single-action mechanisms, meaning that the trigger does only a single thing—it releases the hammer once it is cocked and fires the projectile in a loaded chamber. The trigger does not cock the hammer, which has to be done manually by the operator's thumb. Each time the hammer is cocked back the cylinder rotates and brings a new chamber into battery, while also readying the trigger for firing. Because of this they cannot generally be fired as rapidly as double-action revolvers or automatic pistols. Most of the early designs were similarly limited in the speed they could be reloaded after firing, because they (like the revolvers of Colt and Remington) reloaded through a loading gate cut into the recoil shield behind the cylinder. Once empty, each spent cartridge needed to be ejected with a spring-loaded ejector rod to clear the chambers. Once this was done for each chamber cartridges were loaded one at a time through the open loading gate until the revolver was reloaded. This is much slower than the process for more modern magazine-fed pistols, and meant that some people still tended to carry more than one gun if they knew they were going to get in a fight. Rather than fumble with reloading, once your first weapon was empty you'd drop it and move to something else. But for the time it was a vast improvement on the older cap-and-ball technology.

By the end of the nineteenth century technology moved past the single-action revolver and the limitations of ejector rods and loading gates. Double-action designs were introduced by Colt and other companies, and these set the trend for the future. With a double-action revolver the trigger does two things at once—it rotates the cylinder and fires the hammer, so that the gun can be emptied by pulling the trigger repeatedly. Once the technology was mature double-action revolvers replaced the older single-action designs because they could be fired more rapidly than the earlier single-action guns. In terms of loading, the process was sped by the introduction of top-break designs (first popularized by Smith and Wesson in the 1870s) or swing-out cylinders that ejected all the spent cartridges at once. This made revolvers much easier to load. With special metal clips called "moon clips" certain revolvers could be reloaded with six fresh cartridges in a single motion. Elsewhere "speed loaders" were used to accomplish the same thing. Without these revolvers were still a tad slow to recharge—if you knew you were going to be getting into a gunfight, you might still carry an extra revolver, rather than mess with reloading in the middle of things. During the early part of the twentieth century this practice led to the coining of the term "New York reload," meaning that once you'd emptied your first revolver you'd drop it and grab another.

For most of the twentieth century double-action revolvers of various kinds were the side-arms of choice for both civilians and law enforcement officers. For decades most police forces in the US used six-shot revolvers chambered in .38 Special. These were and are effective and reliable weapons, and even in an age dominated by high-capacity polymer-framed auto pistols a good revolver is an effective means of defense. Even the old single-action "cowboy" guns of the nineteenth century are excellent weapons in the hands of a trained user. A good single-action revolver chambered in .45 Colt is a simple, reliable and effective means of self-defense. They tend to point naturally and allow for intuitive aiming. At short distances where handguns are effective a single-action revolver will stop most fights quickly. Double-action revolvers are likewise superb weapons, reliable, simple, using well-proven technology. These are not obsolete weapons, despite the fact that most police forces, militaries and armed civilians have adopted one of the myriad types of automatic pistols currently in production.

For the zombie apocalypse there are a number of reasons why you might want to start carrying around a revolver. The most important of these regards the reliability of modern (and modern remakes of old designs) revolvers. Compared to automatic pistols, revolvers have relatively few moving parts. They tend to be robustly constructed, and the manual nature of their operation, whether single or double action, ensures that they pretty much always fire whenever they're asked to do so.

If you encounter a defective cartridge, simply pulling the trigger will solve the problem. By nature, revolvers do not jam. That inherent reliability is something to seriously ponder, given that you'll be using your revolver to cut down undead chewers before they start chewing you. Revolvers are easier to maintain than automatic pistols, which may be a serious factor in the apocalypse when keeping things clean may be difficult. If you don't keep your automatic pistol clean it can and will jam on you, costing you precious seconds as you try to clear the jam while rotting office workers creep ever closer to your soft fleshy bits. Revolvers don't jam. Remember it.

If you have access to a model using moon clips or you have speed loaders, revolvers can be reloaded just as quickly as an automatic pistol. As will all things, of course, practice makes perfect. And you'll probably have the opportunity for lots of practice, surrounded as you will be hordes of shambling targets. If you don't have speed loaders or moon clips then you'll need to remember that you can only load a revolver's cylinder so fast—so don't get surrounded and expect to blast your way out with just your six-gun. Speaking of six-guns, the term originated out of the fact that most revolvers carry six rounds in their cylinders. Many smaller models, especially short-barreled (or "snub-nosed") weapons meant for concealment, carry five rounds. Recently there has been something of a fad among several manufacturers for making revolvers that chamber seven or more rounds. Most of what you encounter, though, will chamber only six. Keep that in the back of your mind as you go into battle with the dead masses—once you've fired off the sixth round, you've got reload or run.

Common revolvers chamber a wide range of popular and available ammunition. Revolvers are generally much less finicky about bullet types than automatic pistols are, and will reliably fire off whatever you put in them. Many revolvers also benefit from the ability to fire multiple ammunition types in a way that auto pistols cannot. A 9mm Glock can only fire 9mm Luger. Put 9mm Short in your Glock and you're going to have problems. You're essentially stuck with one type of ammo if you opt for the automatic pistol. A revolver chambered for .357 Magnum, on the other hand, can also chamber .38 Special (which despite the name fires the same diameter bullet as the .357). The difference between the two cartridges is that the .357 has a longer shell casing, and contains more powder. Long-distance accuracy may be affected slightly, since the shorter .38 Special has to travel a longer distance before it gets to the rifling of the barrel, but you won't be doing long-distance target shooting in the zompocalypse. Or at least you won't be doing so with a revolver. Such weapons allow you to take advantage of several types of common ammunition, a valuable thing in aworld where every bullet you fire will be a scavenged bullet. Similarly, revolvers chambered in .44 Magnum (like the iconic Smith & Wesson used by Dirty Harry) can also chamber .44 special. This feature is more important than it seems, at first glance, considering that bullets you cannot fire are worthless to you. Finding a box of rounds for a 10mm automatic doesn't do you much good if you're carrying a 9mm Glock. Revolvers give you more choices.

Revolvers are inherently accurate, because of their fixed barrels. They are capable of firing more powerful cartridges, generally, than automatic pistols, although too much power is overkill, as you know from the comments above regarding the .22 Long Rifle. Limited capacity may be a blessing in disguise, from a certain point of view. If you've ever read Che Guevera's work on guerilla warfare tactics, you'll remember that Guevera championed bolt-action rifles, despite the fact that automatic rifles and other weapons were available. His reasoning was that guerilla soldiers, with their limited resources, would need to fire accurately and make every shot count. Automatic rifles allowed rapid fire, but they tended to make individual soldiers fire repeatedly even when they weren't likely to hit anything. Overall accuracy suffered and too many bullets were being fired. With the limited magazine capacity and rate of fire the soldier with the bolt gun would be forced to make each shot count. The same principle may hold true for zompocalypse survivors armed with revolvers— if you know you've only got six shots, you're more likely to aim carefully and not fire wildly. Data from some police shootings can illustrate this point. In the last decades of the twentieth century police departments across the US began to trade into their .38 caliber revolvers for 9mm automatic pistols that carried many more rounds. What happened during gunfights in the post-revolver period is that many more shots were fired, because there were many more available rounds to be fired. This is one of the reasons why you can read about police shootings where eighty or ninety bullets were fired at a naked guy in a hotel. High capacity automatic pistols can contribute to what's called "spray and pray," whereby the individual in question just starts firing off rounds as fast as possible, hoping that "in the general direction" is good enough. With only six rounds, you need to use them carefully and make each one a hit. This is efficient and it conserves ammunition—remember, any gun without bullets to fire has become a bludgeon. And there are more effective bludgeons, as you know.

Pistols

Even though I spent the last section bashing
automatic pistols (to a certain extent), there's
nothing inherently wrong with them. For defending
yourself against undead hordes, a good quality
automatic pistol would be a fine sidearm. Probably
I haven't stressed enough to this point that it really
isn't the weapon, but the person who uses the
weapon, and how they use it that's the important
thing. Any implement is the right one if it's all
you've got. The battle tactics you use against the
dead are what will keep you alive, not this or that
particular tool. Anyway, automatic pistols are fine
bits of technology that will save your life, against
opponents living and (un)dead.

A bit of history, which you've probably
become accustomed to by now. Automatic pistols
came into their own, so to speak, at the beginning of
the twentieth century. There were a few models
made at the close of the nineteenth century, like the
C96 "Broomhandle" Mauser, but the really
effective, practical designs date to the early
twentieth. Colt again managed to introduce another
iconic design, the 1911 which was the brainchild of
John Browning. Over the years the 1911 has
spawned legions of descendants, with a plethora of
companies producing improved variants of the
design as we speak. The 1911 and its close

relatives operate on a relatively simple principle. Basically, an automatic pistol utilizes the recoil energy generated by firing a cartridge to cycle a mechanical action. With a pull of the trigger the mechanism of an auto pistol unlocks or disengages a bolt, ejecting the now-spent casing at it travels backwards. When the bolt returns due to the action of a powerful spring it strips a fresh cartridge from the top of a spring-loaded magazine and loads it into the gun's breech. With the mechanism returned to battery, another pull of the trigger will repeat the process. An automatic pistol will continue to fire with each pull of the trigger, so long as there are rounds remaining in the magazine. While the designs vary from maker to maker (some are operated via "blow-back," a few are gas-operated) the basic principle remains the same.

Automatic pistols come chambered in a wide variety of calibers, although some are more commonly found than others. Probably the most common chamberings are the venerable 9mm Luger and the .45 ACP. More recently, .40 auto has become popular, especially in law enforcement circles. The Department of Homeland Security recently purchased several hundred million rounds of .40 caliber ammunition to feed the handguns issued by their department. Any or all of these are excellent choices against the walking dead. They are all more than powerful enough to penetrate the slightly-squishy skulls of zombies. All three are very common cartridges, so you'll be able to scrounge some of them up to carry you through the apocalyptic wasteland. If you could only choose one gun from among the multitudinous ranks of modern automatic pistols, a good bet would be to go with the 9mm. Ammunition for 9mm handguns is cheap and plentiful in the world before the apocalypse, and so it will be commonly encountered after the fall of civilization. Handguns chambered in 9mm Luger are common as well. From the point of view of the user, 9mm Luger offers a number of advantages over the more powerful .40 and .45 rounds. First of all, 9mm handguns usually feature light recoil, allowing you faster follow-up shots. If you're fighting a group of zombies, the speed with which you can put them down one after another is more important than the wallop packed by a single round. All three cartridges will penetrate a skull without too much trouble, so lighter recoil is something to think about. The ammunition for your 9mm is relatively small, so you'll be saving space and weight, with the possibility of carrying more ammunition than the other two cartridges. In terms of the guns, common 9mm automatics are capable of holding anywhere from twelve to eighteen cartridges in each magazine. Most 1911-type pistols will only pack seven or eight larger .45 caliber rounds in a magazine. Thus you can put down more zombies without reloading with the smaller 9mm. Against human opponents (bandits should never be discounted) it is true that .40 and .45 rounds seem to pack more of a punch. But 9mm, especially with more powerful modern ammunition and bullet designs, is nothing to sneeze at. Remember, there's no doctor to save you if you catch a 9mm ball round in the stomach. The bandits will be aware of that fact too.

Smaller more-concealable designs exist firing a variety of equally small cartridges—.25 ACP, .32 ACP, .380 Auto. There's nothing wrong with these weapons, necessarily, but you should remember what they were designed for. In the world before the zombie feeding frenzy, civilians with concealed weapons permits needed to be able to conceal the guns they were licensed to carry. Thus an entire subdivision of the firearms industry existed around designing compact weapons that were easy to conceal. Because they needed to be small, they generally chambered low-powered cartridges and carried few rounds in a loaded magazine. Short barrels meant that muzzle velocity (and hence penetration) was negatively affected. This didn't matter, because their intended use was in self-defense scenarios, in which most of the time no shots would be fired. Simply producing the gun would often scare away would-be assailants. Obviously, flashing your tin to a zombie isn't going to have a similar effect. The zombie sees only lunch. With no need to conceal your weapons anymore (again, no law) you should probably relegate smaller handguns to a back-up role and rely on something with a longer barrel and more bullets.

There are a number of automatic pistols built to fire the .22 Long Rifle cartridges that are excellent anti-zombie weapons. Some of the very best of these are made by the Sturm-Ruger corporation. As discussed above, .22 Long Rifle will penetrate the zombie skull, and almost nonexistent recoil means that you'll be able to fire off your rounds accurately. The shells are plentiful and easily carried. Generally .22 caliber automatic pistols are intended for target practice or training, and so they have sufficient weight and barrel length to be easy to use in a zombie gunfight. Do not disrespect the humble .22 LR.

Automatic pistols (and rifles, but we'll get to that below) need to be maintained carefully if you intend them to function reliably. A dirty automatic handgun will inevitably jam due to the fouling produced by firing it. It is only a matter of time. How much time varies considerably from model to model. Many 1911-style handguns have the reputation of being finicky in regards to cleaning and ammo types. Other auto pistols, like the enormously popular Glock designs used by most police departments will continue to function even if they're filthy. But as a general rule of thumb you should keep your auto pistol as clean as you can. Lubricants and solvents necessary to do so will be a priority target of your scavenging. This is a sort of "safety first" argument. While the pistol might be fine, you should still make sure to clean it on a regular schedule according to the frequency of use. A jammed up auto pistol, as you know, is just a bludgeon until the jam is cleared.

Speaking of jamming, since automatic firearms are machines, you'll need to be alright with the fact that sometimes the machines seize up. Most of these malfunctions come in the form of a failure to feed a new cartridge from the magazine. Sometimes ejected shells can get caught in the mechanism, which will interrupt the functioning of the gun. Most jams can be cleared by the manual operation of the weapon's slide, which will hopefully clear the jam and allow another try at loading a new round from the magazine. If you carry any automatic firearm, remember that malfunctions can and will eventually happen. Be prepared, and try to keep yourself and escape route at all times, even when you feel totally in charge of the situation.

A final thing to consider with automatic pistols is in regards to the spring-loaded magazines that feed them. An auto pistol with only one magazine probably has a lower overall rate of fire (as in rounds fired per minute) than a revolver. This is because after the last round is fired from your auto pistol you've got to break the weapon into two separate pieces—the gun and the magazine—and press new rounds into the magazine one at a time against the pressure of a spring. A revolver's cylinder can be quickly emptied and reloaded immediately, without fighting against a spring. The high rate of fire of automatic pistols is deceptive, because it relies upon extra loaded magazines. Pick up an abandoned Glock and you're a lot better off than when you used a kitchen knife to fight clear of your apartment. But with only that single magazine you've actually got a very limited firing time. Reloading your Glock's magazine as a group of zombies shambles hungrily in your direction is not a situation you want to be in. Where possible, get extra magazines. In a scavenging situation, you're better off with the most common models of auto pistol, so 1911s and 9mm Glocks are good choices. Each one you find gives you an extra magazine. In that sense, once you've got the gun the extra magazines are more valuable to you than the extra gun is.

Submachine Guns

For some reason popular culture has the tendency to label any fully automatic weapon a "machine gun." This is incorrect. Machine guns are large, heavy, usually belt-fed infantry support weapons. A submachine gun is something quite different. The first submachine guns found their inspiration in the tactical stalemate of the First World War. Infantry of the time simply didn't have enough firepower to assault defended trench systems and make much of an impact. Submachine guns were born of the idea that if you could give a single soldier a portable, controllable automatic weapon he could sweep through a trench system and win a foot-hold for other soldiers to follow. These weapons were designed to use pistol-caliber ammunition and spring-loaded box magazines. They operated like automatic pistols, but expended their ammunition continuously so long as the trigger was depressed. Thus they were fully automatic.

The Thompson Submachine gun is probably one of the more famous designs, because it was linked with the Depression-era crime wave that swept through America after the end of the First World War. Gangsters fighting over bootlegging territory and bank robbers involved in heavily-armed daylight robberies appreciated the Thompson's ferocious rate of fire. It spat out the same powerful slugs fired by the Colt 1911, and it fired a lot of them very fast. It was even somewhat controllable, despite the fully automatic rate of fire. They were also scary weapons to be on the receiving end of—a Thompson in action belches out a massive fireball from its relatively short barrel, so those down range had their senses assaulted in terms of both sight and sound. Those weapons equipped with fifty-round drum magazines were capable of long bursts of fire. This was the weapon that "made the twenties roar."

Submachine guns, including the Thompson, featured heavily in the fighting of the Second World War. They provided heavy short-range firepower, and were deadly in house-to-house fighting, and anywhere else where terrain put troops into close contact with one another. In Stalingrad the Soviet army made heavy use of the Ppsh 41, a simple, rugged submachine gun that fired a high velocity 7.62mm round. It was so heavily used that it became an iconic symbol on Soviet propaganda posters. For their intended purpose, these were excellent weapons.

Fully automatic submachine guns are going to be extremely rare, due to restrictions on the ownership of such weapons. Semi-automatic variants, that fire a single round with each pull of the trigger, will occasionally be encountered, and there's no reason that these would be a poor choice. They are essentially a large, more controllable auto pistol, with a longer barrel and site radius. The pistol cartridges they fire are as common as for the automatic pistols, and their longer barrels means higher velocity and greater accuracy. You lack the fully automatic feature of the military-grade models, but that's of little use to you against the undead. The loss of control and high expenditure of ammunition under fully automatic fire is a liability against zombies. While a burst of fire might shred a human opponent, that same burst will probably inflict only meaningless flesh wounds on a zombie. In general, fully automatic fire is always to be avoided.

As with automatic pistols, the availability of magazines is off crucial importance. Your semi-automatic Uzi or Thompson will fire the twenty or thirty rounds contained in its magazine, and then you're reloading the thing one round at a time. Even worse than auto pistols, you'll be struggling with your relatively heavy and bulky submachine gun while you load one cartridge at a time into the magazine, trying to keep one eye on the zombie reinforcements creeping up on you. Also worse than auto pistols, the rarity of your Thompson or Uzi (or Sten or whichever make you have) means that you're not going to find many extra magazines. This makes submachine guns much less useful to you in the changed world of the zombie apocalypse. There are worse choices, but there are many better ones also. Keep in mind the benefits and limitations of submachine guns, and remember that zombies know no fear and cannot feel pain.

The Shotgun

Perhaps it is no wonder that according to popular culture the shotgun is the pinnacle of anti-zombie technology. They are common, and they are effective. That is, they are common because they are staple of both the hunting and the self-defense subcultures of the US firearms industry, and because they are technologically simple and therefore inexpensive. As with everything else in the modern US (and elsewhere) ubiquity is closely associated with the cost of manufacture and the subsequent profit to be made from a sale.

In these respects shotguns have a lot to recommend them. They are cheap to make, and they are effective once they are made. Shotguns are everywhere, and even people who know next to nothing about firearms are familiar with shotguns. Once the zombie apocalypse starts, shotguns of various makes and models will be commonly encountered weapons, and so they should be discussed here, despite that fact that I've spent a certain amount of time denigrating them above.

First, a bit of history. The idea of a shotgun is of considerable antiquity, really. The very first black powder firearms were smoothbore weapons that could more or less launch anything that was stuffed down their barrels. In certain circumstances that meant that anything that was available was thrust down the muzzle of a cannon or a handheld blunderbuss and fired at some nameless enemy. The blunderbuss, as it is known today, was essentially the first self-defense shotgun. In appearance they look like a shortened, mutant version of the run-of-the-mill military musket—a short barrel, with a massive bell-shaped muzzle and large bore. A blunderbuss was not meant for marksmanship or hunting. It was instead designed for the short-range slaughter of enemy soldiers or sailors. The large bore and the lack of rifling meant that it could fire pretty much anything that was stuffed down its maw—rocks, nails, coins, chopped up musket balls, bird shot, dinner ware, buttons—no matter the fodder it would send it downrange. The blunderbuss was an especially effective weapon in naval warfare, since man-to-man combat was always at close range due to the confines of contemporary sailing vessels. There the lack of accuracy meant little, and the indiscriminant spread of projectiles from the weapon meant that you had a greater chance of striking the enemy. With only a single shot, this was not something to discount.

In the American West shotguns were effectively used both in law enforcement circles and for hunting and civilian self defense. Shotguns (these were all double-barreled designs, with only two shots, one in each of two barrels) were everywhere. They were simple, reliable, durable, and effective. They were useful hunting tools. They were effective for short-range self defense. They were so simple mechanically that you pretty much never had to worry about them malfunctioning. The shotgun was the unsung hero of frontier firearms. While the Colt revolver got all the press the humble double-barreled shotgun guarded the farms and trains and stagecoaches of nineteenth century American society. While the dime novels of the time wrote about six-gun duels and dramatic European style fights over honor on an American stage, real bandits and gunfighters used shotguns as the ultimate short-range weapons, the tool that decided gunfights, bank robberies and stagecoach holdups. The six-shooter was dramatic and sexy. The double-barreled shotgun was so intimidating and lethal that resistance was futile.

By the end of the nineteenth century repeating magazine-fed shotguns began to supplement the more traditional break-open double-barreled designs. Winchester was a pioneer in this respect, introducing a lever-action shotgun in the late 1880s, and a pump-action model a decade later. The design of pump-action shotguns has varied relatively little since the end of the nineteenth century, with modern pump guns working along essentially the same principles. These weapons fed (and feed) from a tubular spring-loaded magazine that holds anywhere from three to eight shells. Each time a pump shotgun's slide is worked, it ejects an empty shell and loads another from the magazine. These weapons will fire as long as there are shells in the magazine, and the magazines can be "topped off" with additional shells while the weapon remains in operation. Shotguns have been used as specialized weapons for close combat by both law enforcement and military personnel for more than a century. They are effective and easy to operate.

The principal feature that distinguishes shotguns from other small arms is the nature of their ammunition. Shotguns have smooth-bore barrels, and so they can fire multiple projectiles at once. This makes them more dangerous at close range. In Napoleonic times the flintlock military musket was also smooth bored, and so soldiers sometimes cut up musket balls into smaller pieces or fired purpose-built "buck and ball" cartridges to maximize their lethality at close range. In that sense a pump-action shotgun is nothing more than a repeating musket—they have large bores and can fire a blast of bird or buckshot in order to serve different purposes. With small birdshot a shotgun is the weapon of choice for hunting fowl. Loaded with larger buckshot they are lethal close-range weapons for soldiers, police forces, and civilian self defense. There are even solid slugs that really do make the shotgun into a reasonably accurate repeating musket. They are versatile weapons.

Against people shotguns are highly effective weapons. At close range there is little that is deadlier than a properly loaded shotgun firing the right size of buckshot. Their effects are so lethal that the distinctive sound of a pump-action shotgun being cycled is in itself a deterrent to would-be attackers. The possibility of being shredded by half a dozen whizzing projectiles is something nobody wants to face, if they have a choice. Shotguns will stop a fight, if it starts. They will also stop it from starting in the first place, due to the psychological impact associated their appearance and reputation. They are indeed deadly weapons.

In a world dominated by zombies they are still effective, but there are a number of important issues to consider. Certainly shotguns retain their lethality and their psychological impact against bandits or cannibals. Such individuals are as vulnerable to a shotgun blast as they were in the time before the apocalypse, and even more so, considering the lack of working trauma centers. If getting shot once is bad, catching a belly full or limb full of buckshot or birdshot is worse. Nobody, even the most nutty cannibal, is going to want to catch the wrath of a shotgun.

While shotguns are a staple of zombie warfare in film and in popular culture, there are a number of serious drawbacks to relying on a shotgun. While the weapons and the shells they load are incredibly common, they are also bulky. Remember the musket connection? The big single-shot muskets used by Napoleonic soldiers were loaded with paper cartridges roughly the same size as a shotgun shell. Soldiers carried these fragile cartridges in cartridge boxes attached to their belts. Generally an individual would carry thirty or forty cartridges—they were heavy and bulky, and when these ran out more would be obtained from supplies on hand. In a world ruled by hordes of the undead there are no quartermasters to help resupply your automatic musket. Those thirty or forty shells you're carrying around for your twelve gauge will take up a lot of space. They're also heavy. This means that you can only carry so many on your person. Against human opponents thirty or forty shotgun shells is an enormous pile of ammunition. One or two will do. In the zompocalypse you're going to face a lot more than thirty or forty opponents. You will never have too much ammunition. The bulk and weight of shotgun shells are almost a deal breaker, at least at the level of the lone survivor. If you have a strong group or a well-defended (or hidden) home base, then things change a bit. If you're not carrying everything on your back, weight and space become less important. Just remember that if you choose a shotgun, you won't be carrying hundreds of rounds of ammunition on your person.

The possibility of friendly-fire notwithstanding, shotguns have the potential for considerable overkill. Zombies can be taken down by a single .22 Long Rifle round. Blasting nine pellets (as in 00 buckshot) out of your shotgun has the potential to waste metal, and it definitely wastes powder. The heavy recoil of a shotgun will send multiple projectiles down range, but many or most (or all) of these may miss the zombie brain that is your target. The flesh wounds and bleeding shotguns inflict on humans—the things that quickly end the fight in the favor of the shotgunner—are worthless against the undead. You can liberally spray a zombie with buckshot and fail to stop it, if the brain and spinal column remains intact.

Realize also that the seven or eight rounds in your shotgun must be reloaded one at a time through a loading gate. There is no quick-change magazine (a few relatively rare designs do utilize spring-loaded box or drum magazines, but most shotguns you'll encounter will be either double-barreled designs or the ubiquitous pump-action models). Each blast of the shotgun is one shell closer to the dreaded "click!" that you should hear as "run!"

Lever Action Rifles

The first effective repeating rifles were developed in the middle of the nineteenth century. The most popular designs were those produced by Winchester, whose operation (similar to pump-action shotguns) relied upon a tubular under-barrel magazine. Once loaded with a dozen (or more) .44 or .45 caliber rounds the weapon could be fired repeatedly, with each cycling of the action ejecting a spend cartridge and loading a new one from the magazine. This was accomplished via the working of a lever that protruded below the action and formed the weapon's trigger guard. These rifles fired pistol-caliber cartridges, and so were limited to a fairly short range, by the standards of period single-shot rifles. Past a couple of hundred yards the loss of velocity made it difficult to hit a target, and reduced the lethality of the projectile. At closer ranges, however, they were deadly. Lever action rifles in .44-40 or .45 Colt were the assault weapons of the late nineteenth century, capable of a high rate of fire and good accuracy. The rounds they fired were lethal to humans at reasonable distances, with the soft-lead bullets expanding as they penetrated a target.

Many kinds of modern lever action rifles are produced today. Some have updated design features, while others are more or less exact copies of the models popular in the nineteenth century. They are simple to use and reliable. They fire relatively common types of ammunition (indeed, you can find them chambering .38 Special, .357 Magnum, .45 Colt, .44 Magnum, and others). Their iron sights are capable of decent accuracy. It should be kept in mind that like the shotgun they load only a single round at a time, most of them through a loading gate on the right hand side of the weapon. You'll need to watch your back and be careful not to get trapped with an unloaded rifle.

Unlike shotguns, the ammunition fired by lever action rifles (alright, most of them...some fire larger, bulkier cartridges) is fairly light and compact. With a little luck you'll be able to find a revolver that chambers the same cartridge as your lever gun, easing your supply problems. Remember that every round that protects you from the zombie horde is a round that must be scavenged.

"Assault" Rifles

So-called assault weapons are highly controversial firearms. In the US their role in recent incidents of mass murder has once again brought them into the political limelight, where proponents of gun control attack them as unnecessary tools of destruction that have no place in a civilized society. On the other side of the debate pro-gun groups defend these as essentially the same as other firearms, and that calls for bans on assault weapons will inevitably lead to further bans.

Elsewhere in the world, what Americans refer to with the term assault weapons are either very common or almost non-existent, depending on the particular place. An Indian colleague of mine recently told me that while guns are relatively common in India (legal and illegal), assault rifles are not, and are usually a sign that the holder is an opponent of the government. That is, the bearer of an AK-47 isn't just well armed, he's making a political statement. In many places assault rifles are entirely the province of the military, and are not allowed in civilian hands. This volume is not going to delve into the passionate arguments about the place of assault weapons in modern society—you can find an endless mass of partisan writings on the subject, from all sides of the political spectrum. If you aren't in the US, you can look in from the outside and shake your head at gun-loving Americans. In any event this volume is dedicated to discussing weapons and warfare as both subjects relate to a zombie apocalypse. And regardless of how you feel about firearms, when the zombies rise arguments about the place of firearms will be pointless.

Exactly what anti-gun exponents mean by assault weapons is not particularly well-defined, largely because anti-gun groups don't usually know that much about firearms or the history of firearms. For example, any appropriate shoulder-fired weapon with sufficient ammunition capacity might be considered an assault weapon, if it can be used in battle. An 1873 Winchester lever-action rifle was an assault weapon in the nineteenth century, and it would actually do a pretty good job in a fight even in modern times. The cartridges are effective at short range, and so forth. Pump action shotguns are also sometimes used by military forces as specialized assault weapons. The term "assault weapon" is problematic.

If by assault weapon an individual is referring to an automatic gas or piston operated rifle firing a moderately powerful cartridge, then they're looking at something more specific and distinct. Historically such weapons were born during the carnage of the Second World War. Semi-automatic battle rifles firing full-power rifle cartridges were fielded by many of the military forces engaged in the conflict, notably the armed forces of Soviet Russia, Germany, and the United States. But it was the Germans who took things further, inventing the first "assault rifle" in the process of their war with Russia. The Germans were involved in a number of brutal long-term sieges on the Eastern Front, where urban warfare put a premium on close range firepower. Submachine guns went a long way towards providing this, but the pistol cartridges such weapons fired lacked accuracy and stopping power at anything other than close range. The German military looked for a solution to the problem, trying to find a weapon that would give soldiers lots of firepower up close while still allowing them to be effective at longer ranges. This resulted in the creation of the Sturmgewehr 44, an automatic rifle that fired a .30 caliber cartridge and fed from a box magazine. What was really innovative about the Sturmgewehr 44 was not the gun itself, which shared features with other period automatic rifles. The interesting thing was the cartridge, which was not a full blown rifle cartridge, but instead was shortened and contained less propellant. This intermediate rifle round was more powerful than the pistol calibers of the submachine guns, but less powerful than the rounds rifles by other military rifles. The less powerful cartridge of the Sturmgewehr resulted in less recoil, which allowed more controllable fully automatic fire, while retaining enough power to be effective at longer ranges. The designers had to actually shroud their design in secrecy, since Hitler opposed the weapon's construction. Once it was issued, however, it was so well liked by the soldiers that production was increased and more were ordered for the conflict in the east.

The next episode in the story of the assault rifle involves the Russians, who were on the receiving end of the German designs and learned from them. In 1947 a Russian tank mechanic (and later tank commander) named Mikhail Kalashnikov created arguably the most famous (or infamous) rifle design of the last half-century. This was the AK-47. Continuously improved from decade to decade, it and its progeny are the most common military weapons in the world. Cheap to produce, simple enough that anyone can use it, the AK-47 is one of the most prolific weapons in the history of armed conflict. Produced in huge numbers by the Soviets and later Communist China, they are everywhere in the world, used by militaries, militias, rebels, criminals and everyone in between.

All modern militaries equip their front line troops with some form of assault rifle. Many of them are capable of fully automatic fire, though this is sparingly used by most soldiers because of the speed with which it can exhaust ammunition. In combat most assault rifles are used to fire short bursts or aimed single shots. Fully automatic fire is usually relegated to suppression. Modern assault rifles have not changed in any substantial way from the first designs introduced by the Germans and Russians in the middle of the twentieth century. They remain magazine-fed rifles firing a moderately powerful rifle cartridge.

Assault rifles are a useful tool for surviving the zombie apocalypse. The ammunition fired by these weapons is relatively light, and quite a few rounds can be carried on an individual's person. In the US such weapons are commonly carried not only by Army and National Guard forces but also by law enforcement agencies. The increased militarization of America's police forces is something to be concerned about, depending on your political beliefs—but after the dead rise the fact that most police forces have a certain number of M4 assault rifles in their arsenals will be a good thing. Overrun military positions are also likely to yield abandoned assault rifles. The common nature of these weapons, much more than submachine guns, means that eventually the average zompocalypse survivor should be able to locate an assault rifle and several extra magazines. There are enough M4 and AK style automatic rifles in civilian hands, moreover, that finding these shouldn't be too much trouble. Civilian models will not be capable of fully automatic fire, but you won't be using that anyway, since it is only a useless waste of ammunition. Save your bullets and make every shot count.

Against zombies an assault rifle is a powerful weapon. The large magazine capacities allow the user to engage groups of zombies. The rounds are more than powerful enough to pierce the zombie skull, and recoil is light enough that fast follow-up shots are possible. There is a reason why these weapons have replaced more powerful rifles in all the world's military forces. They are effective at what they were designed to do. Against human bandits (as always, safety first) assault rifles are equally potent. The lack of medical care mentioned previously applies to the high-velocity rounds fired by modern assault rifles—anyone getting struck by these rounds is unlikely to survive long without medical attention, even if the wound fails to immediately incapacitate and kill.

The rate of fire these weapons are capable of is something to carefully consider in the changed world of the zombie apocalypse. Remembering that every round must be scavenged, the assault rifle operator must remember that even the civilian semi-automatic models are capable of firing off ammunition very quickly. The ability to fire very fast needs to be used very carefully—under the effects of fear a lone survivor might fire too many bullets in a panic. As with every other firearm, when there are no bullets to fire assault rifles become bludgeons.

Some assault rifles come equipped with bayonet lugs. Most of these are military variants, and many militaries continue to issue bayonets to their soldiers. In modern warfare bayonets are nearly useless as weapons, due to the ubiquity of automatic rifles and machineguns. But the rules change once the dead rise. Against slow zombie attackers an assault rifle with a bayonet becomes a powerful and multi-functional tool, capable of cutting down zombies at any effective combat distance. As with any type of close combat, caution must be used. To get within bayonet range, you're getting dangerously close the lethal smile of your zombified opponent.

Bolt Action Rifles

Bolt action rifles were the military weapon of choice through the first half of the twentieth century. They had lots of things to recommend them for such a role. Their powerful cartridges, almost universally some form of .30 caliber round, meant that they were capable of lethal fire out to very long distances. The bolt actions themselves were very sturdy designs that held up well to the hard use common to twentieth century battlefields. When used by a group of soldiers fighting together bolt action rifles were capable of a high enough rate of fire to break an infantry assault. At the same time, their bolt operation and inherent accuracy prompted the soldier to fire carefully, which worked to conserve ammunition supplies.

As hunting weapons bolt action rifles are extremely common, with those manufactured by Remington probably the most prolifically made. Most bolt action hunting rifles fire a .30 cartridge of some kind, and feed from an internal spring-loaded magazine. Rounds must be loaded individually on most civilian models, with the bolt opened to gain access to the magazine plate. Military rifles from the period of the two World Wars loaded with "stripper clips," small metal clips which loaded a number of rounds (usually five) at once. This made reloading faster and allowed the soldier to keep up a constant rate of fire. Unless you've got one of these weapons (and the loaded clips), loading a bolt action rifle is relatively slow.

Bolt-action rifles make up for their low magazine capacity and rate of fire by being very powerful and very accurate. These are the features that explain their popularity as hunting weapons. Most bolt action rifles as designed to be used with rifle scopes, telescopic sighting devices that allow accurate fire at long ranges. Essentially they are sniper weapons.

Against zombies the many makes of bolt-action rifles are effective tools for specialized anti-zombie missions. They are not meant to be used at close range, but rather to provide accurate fire at distance. Stationary or slowly shambling zombie heads can be popped with a bolt-action rifle at great distances. The user can remain entirely safe while he picks off zombies one after another. The one drawback of this "sniper solution" is that without suppressors the powerful cartridges used by bolt-action rifles are very loud. If you get too enthusiastic about blasting zombified pedestrians you'll notice that the report of your sniper rifle tends to draw in new zombies from afar. If destroying fifteen zombies draws in a hundred more to the sound of your rifle fire, you've got a problem. This factor is an issue with any firearm, really, but the report of a potent bolt-action rifle is particularly loud, and even more effective at drawing in additional attackers.

Similarly, the loud report of bolt guns will alert every potentially dangerous human in the vicinity to your location. They'll know you're armed, of course, but will have some idea of where you are. It's hard to be anonymous with a bolt-action rifle. Against humans a bolt-action rifle is obviously lethal, but not well suited to close range combat. Whatever the opponent, you'll need to consider the specialized nature of your weapon, and keep your enemies at long range where a telescopic sight and extreme accuracy are useful. Caution is the key.

Explosives

Explosives have been used as weapons long before there was anything that could be described as a firearm. The ancient Chinese used gunpowder in various kinds of bombs and explosive devices for centuries before anyone thought about using the propellant to launch a projectile at a foe. The reason is simple, in that simplicity is the hallmark of crude explosive devices. Simply fill a container that restricts expanding gases with some kind of explosive, and provide for a fuse, and you have an explosive. Explosive devices are scary, and indiscriminate. The reports of soldiers from the First and Second World Wars more or less always list artillery fire or mortars as being far more frightening than bullets. An explosion is hard to escape from.

As an anti-zombie weapon, explosive devices are mixed in their effectiveness. The nature of zombies, both their psychology (or lack thereof) and physiology, means that survivors will need to carefully employ explosives, if they decide to use them. As always, safety is a prime concern, as there will generally be no doctor or surgeon to help you deal with errant grenade or bomb fragments.

Contrary to some popular opinions, explosives are not completely ineffective against the undead. Due to the unique nature of zombie physiology, zombies are not as vulnerable to bombs and explosives as people are. But they are not immune either.

Explosions kill and wound by a combination of fragmentation and blast. Fragmentation refers to the scatter of shrapnel and bits of surrounding material thrown outward by the explosive force of an explosion. These projectiles are not aerodynamic, being that they are not uniformly shaped, and the projectile fragments lose energy relatively quickly and don't have as long an effective range as aerodynamic projectiles such as bullets. But within the danger zone of the explosion they are deadly. The basic concept behind fragmentation grenades, carried by the soldiers of most armies, is that the blast will cause a lethal blast of shrapnel that will shred nearby soldiers. Those not killed or incapacitated by the fragmentation will likely be disorientated by the blast of the explosion itself. Blast refers to the pressure wave, essentially compressed air, that surges outward from the epicenter of an explosion. In most movies and popular culture more generally blast is not given anywhere near the respect it deserves. Explosive blast is not something that knocks the hero (cop, soldier, whatever) dramatically through the air, to land essentially unharmed. Instead, it is a lethal wall of force that can liquefy internal organs and crush the fragile organism that is the human body. The more powerful the explosion, the more dramatic is the effect of the explosive blast wave. During the siege of the Port Arthur in the Russo-Japanese War (1904-1905), for instance, the repeated blast waves of artillery shells were so powerful that they flattened bodies like grotesque pancakes. Blast waves are terrifying.

Most hand-held explosives are not powerful enough to create really massive pressure waves, but there are some exceptions. Dynamite, while somewhat unstable, is capable of producing fairly impressive blast waves. Get enough of it, and it is more than capable of ripping a human body apart. And thus it does have some utility where anti-zombie warfare is concerned. As with all other weapons, the essential point always revolves back to the basic underpinning of zombie physiology. Zombies are undead humans, but the human form is still more or less the same. They require intact bones and muscles to ambulate, an intact jaw structure to bite, and a whole spinal column to continue their body's operation. Explosives, if powerful enough, can most definitely disrupt these organic systems. An explosion that doesn't destroy a zombie is still capable of inflicting enough damage to the skeletal system (and the muscles that provide motive force) to cripple it. A hand grenade or some carefully placed dynamite may result in enough damage to destroy or cripple a number of undead opponents. As with anything else, the survivor is urged to remain as flexible and resourceful as possible at all times. Use your superior speed and intellect, as these things are your greatest advantages against the zombie hordes. Weapons, whether these are guns or knives or bundles of dynamite, are simply tools that you use to stay alive. The most important factor is not the weapon itself but how it is employed.

Perhaps the most useful application of explosives to anti-zombie combat operations involves their use in ambushes. This is especially true in urban areas where buildings can supply traps for both zombies and the pressure effects caused by explosions. Lure a band of shambling zombies into a dead end alley and climb away to escape, and you've got a bunch of undead bodies waiting to be ripped apart by a well chosen explosive device. Whether this is something specially rigged beforehand or something carried on your person, explosives are not worthless against zombies in such a situation. Remember that while maimed zombies are not destroyed they are potentially crippled to the extent that they are much less dangerous than an intact specimen. A zombie with crushed legs and burst eyes is going to be less effective at finding and noshing on you than a newly-turned office worker with all his or her component parts in full working order. Zombie warfare is about thinning the herd and living to fight another day. Whatever you do to survive, one of the most important things to remember is that no matter how deadly you become to the zombie hordes you are still and always will be hopelessly outnumbered. Combat with the undead in an apocalyptic scenario is a series of delaying actions and ambushes—set-piece battles will win you only local victories.

Flame

     The use of fire as a weapon has a long and varied history. The Chinese used various types of incendiary devices on the battlefield for centuries. Mostly these were deployed as some type of fire bomb, although the Chinese did develop a type of early flamethrower. The Byzantine Empire famously manufactured a variety of flame throwers and bombs using an incendiary liquid known as "Greek Fire." The recipe for making this compound was a state secret of the Byzantines, which they kept so well that we don't know exactly what it was made of. Greek Fire probably included some form of petroleum, obtained by accessing surface deposits of the stuff in what is now the state of Turkey. Both the Byzantine and Chinese flamethrowers were conceptually simple. In these ancient flamethrowers a piston would be pulled back, drawing in an amount of viscous flammable liquid, which would be mixed with oxygen. When the piston was then compressed the liquid was sprayed outwards from a nozzle in the front of the device, across a flaming wick that would ignite the spray. The range of these devices was quite short, but for their time they were highly effective. Ship-mounted flame projectors annihilated both Viking and Arab invasion fleets over the course of Byzantine history, and thus they were responsible for playing an important role in protecting

Constantinople from its enemies. Against wooden ships fire projectors were absolutely lethal.

In the twentieth century flamethrowers were adopted by most modern militaries. These weapons were special-purpose instruments meant to dislodge or kill enemy entrenched enemy soldiers. Using a compressed mixture of propellant gases and thickened gasoline, flamethrowers were introduced in the First World War and used in the trench warfare that defined that conflict. In the Second World War the weapons were used to destroy pillboxes and other hardened emplacements when conventional weapons were ineffective. The extreme temperatures of the ignited gas mixture meant that victims of the flames suffered a ghastly and horrifying death. As such, the weapons and their operators were generally despised and rarely extended any mercy by the opposing side. Normally, flamethrower operators would wind up being executed if they were unfortunate enough to fall into enemy hands. Flamethrowers continued to be used by the US in the Korean and Vietnam conflicts, both as infantry weapons and mounted on tanks or other vehicles. In 1978 the US abandoned the use of flamethrowers, partially due to the bad press attached to the devices and partially because their short battlefield range made them only marginally useful on the modern battlefield.

Most zompocalypse survivors will be familiar with flame projector weapons from watching movies that depict their use. The problem with these depictions is that most films don't use real flamethrowers, which project jellied gasoline. Instead, they show flame weapons that fire ignited propane or compressed natural gas, which is much safer for the actors involved in filming than the napalm launched out of the real thing. Military-grade flamethrowers are capable of projecting a stream of napalm out to about 50-80 meters from the nozzle. The extremely high temperatures of the flaming liquid make flamethrowers a terrifying and effective weapon against people.

Against zombies, they are not as effective. First, one of the great advantages of the flamethrower is that it is really scary to have to face down the nozzle of an enemy using it against you. The human mind is fully capable of anticipating what it might be like to be caught alight by an incandescent stream of burning liquid. Nobody wants to be burned alive, and that is basically what flamethrowers do to their victims. Zombies, being zombies, don't have the capacity for fear and so they don't fear being burned a-dead. Also, they can't feel pain, which means that they won't dance around and gurgle as they cook, as a human would. They continue to move forward. The best that can be hoped for is that the zombie's remaining sensory organs are damaged by the intense heat of the flames. A zombie with melted eyes and burnt up nasal passages and eardrums isn't going to be as effective at locating you. It might shamble around aimlessly, unable to locate anything to feast upon. But it won't be destroyed, at least not quickly. Not that this level of incapacitation is for military-grade flamethrowers of the type used during the wars of the twentieth century. The most pressing problem with flamethrowers is that you almost certainly won't be able to find one. Even if you did, such weapons use specialized fuel that sprays out very quickly. Even a fully-charged flamethrower is unlikely to be much more than a brief novelty to zompocalypse survivors. They are too rare, and their fuel runs out too fast.

Of course there are other flame weapons besides flamethrowers. Probably one of the most well-known flame weapons is the incendiary bomb known as a "Molotov Cocktails." The name was coined by the Finns, taken from the Soviet Foreign Minister Vyacheslav Molotov, who was responsible for the Soviet invasion of Finland in what is known as the Winter War (1939-1940). During that conflict the outnumbered Finns used gasoline bombs as anti-tank weapons, often to great effect. These were simple devices, with a glass container holding a measure of adulterated (usually thickened) gasoline, with a cloth wick for a fuse. Later designs used chemical ignition or large matches lashed to the outside of the container, much safer ignition systems for the user than the flaming wicks of the first Molotov cocktails. Tanks of the time were vulnerable because the burning gasoline mixture could penetrate into the engine compartment and ignite fuel or ammunition supplies. Barring that, if the flames or fumes were sucked into the body of the tank (air was usually drawn into the crew compartments from outside) then the crew would either suffocate or abandon their compromised vehicle.

Molotov cocktails are simple weapons to manufacture, though they are somewhat dangerous to use. The problem with using them as anti-zombie weapons is that they lack the capacity to quickly destroy the undead. A flaming zombie might suffer damage to its remaining sensory organs, but if they can still search you out they'll be even more dangerous, being that they're now moving torches. Molotov cocktails are of more use against human enemies and the vehicles they might utilize. So despite their limited utility the concept of the Molotov cocktail and its historical usage should be filed away in the back of your mind with the rest of your zombie survival catalogue. You never know when a piece of seemingly obscure knowledge will come in handy, once society collapses.

Battering Ram: Vehicles as Weapons

Car accidents kill tens of thousands of people a year in the US alone. Living humans are highly susceptible to the sudden deceleration that occurs in a car accident, and our bodies are fragile enough that we can easily incur fatal injuries. Zombies are much more resilient in regards to the amount of physical punishment they can take and continue to function, but they still share the same physical structure. All a zombie is, after all, is a bunch of bones being propelled by a set of more-or-less functioning muscles. Smash the mechanism that is the zombie body, and it will be much less of a threat to you. You might not destroy a zombie by ramming it with a car (or other large machine) but you are very likely to mangle it enough that it ceases to be an immediate threat.

Cars and gasoline should be readily available after the fall of civilization, with a certain amount of requisite scrounging. Long streams of stalled cars jammed onto a highway are unlikely to all be empty of gasoline, all at once. A simple length of hose or tube will allow you to siphon gas from most cars and trucks without too much trouble. As for the vehicles themselves, you don't necessarily need to know how to hot-wire a vehicle, as there will be cars here and there with the keys already provided, ready and waiting in the ignition.

Imagine a traffic jam on a major arterial or a local freeway as it is overrun by a band of walking corpses. In the initial stages of the apocalyptic breakdown of society zombies will be even more terrifying than in the later stages, because survivors will have grown somewhat familiar with them and learned how to fight back and survive. Terrified motorists stalled on a highway, unsure of what is happening, are going to be very likely to panic. Panicked people aren't going to stick around to get eaten. They will abandon their vehicles, many of them, and run away in a big frightened mob that will most likely be devoured later on or be killed off by the elements/reactionary government forces/scared fellow survivors, etc. The panic of the initial disaster will result in quite a few vehicles with available keys.

Cars and trucks are obviously great for transporting you and your scavenged stuff around the countryside, and they can provide a moderately secure sleeping space in unknown territory. They suffer from the drawback of making noise, which can potentially attract both zombies and humans interested in helping themselves to your belongings (or you, in various creepy ways). Vehicles are also limited by the types of terrain they can pass over, depending on your choice of vehicle. Your trusty Honda isn't going to fare very well as an off-road vehicle, so you should make your choice with the types of driving you might anticipate. It is also worth noting that many of the major roadways are likely to be blocked by stalled cars or blockaded by the first survivors (or government military forces) from the early days of the apocalypse. As a post-apocalyptic motorist you'll have to be adaptable.

Vehicles are clearly useful to survival in the apocalypse, but this section is most interested in a specialized use of vehicles—that is, as weapons of zombie warfare. What follows is a discussion of the tactical uses of cars and trucks as weapons.

Vehicular assault is effective against zombies for the same reason cars and trucks are dangerous to people—they're several thousand pounds of metal, rubber and plastic, all of it moving at high speed. Individual zombies and small groups are fair game for vehicular zombie-cide, depending on the numbers arrayed against you and the particular type of vehicle you find yourself in. As with anything else a certain amount of caution is called for. Don't plunge your Honda into a sea of several hundred zombies and expect that everything will be fine. Pretty much any vehicle will be bogged down if there are enough zombies to squish under the tires, and being marooned amid a sea of ravenous corpses is a death sentence, one way or the other. Either you'll die of thirst, trapped inside your conveyance, or the zombies will find some way to batter their way inside and you'll end up as a hot lunch.

Not all cars and trucks are created equally, as far as using them as manned projectiles is concerned. Cars are obviously less effective, generally, given their smaller mass and less-rugged construction. Also note that the lower body line of cars means that the vulnerable windows are easily accessible to zombie limbs. But if you need to, or you have no other choice, a car will mangle zombies quite effectively.

The best kind of everyday civilian vehicle to consider for service as a weapon is a truck or SUV equipped with a snow plow or a large winch bumper. These vehicles are more or less armored to the front, and should stand up to the rigors of splattering zombies very well. Fuel economy is more of a concern with trucks, but with some forethought you should be able to overcome that minor limitation. Trucks and SUVs are also higher off the ground, with windows that are less vulnerable to zombie attempts at joining you in the front seat. With a bit of ingenuity you should be able to armor the windows (if you've got some time and access to a hardware or home-improvement store), making your specialized vehicle even more resistant.

Zombies, as you should realize by now, won't generally be destroyed by ramming them with a car or truck. But they will be damaged to a greater or less extent. Their skeletal system is every bit as vulnerable to being fractured and crushed as yours is, and a mostly-crushed zombie is going to be much less effective at chasing after you. The tactical use of vehicles in regard to zombies is as a form of initial assault, with the vehicle being used as a large projectile to break up groups of zombies and maim individuals to the point of incapacitation. Speed should be varied depending on the situation, but you shouldn't go fast enough to totally wreck your car or truck. You're trying to break bones and squish zombies underneath your tires, not splatter them into paste. It is probably also worth disabling airbags, if your car or truck is equipped with them.

Military grade vehicles, while generally suffering from terrible fuel economy and being relatively harder to find are excellent choices. They are manufactured to resist small-arms fire and all the other hazards of rough military use, and so they'll stand up better to the battering that results from crushing zombies.

If you have the appropriate specialized knowledge and the available fuel, a much more specialized type of vehicle for destroying zombies comes in a form you probably haven't thought of yet—that of heavy construction equipment. These are not getaway vehicles, obviously, and they are not necessarily simple to pilot, but if you have the skill these behemoth machines can certainly rend a gory path through the ranks of the undead. Bulldozers, front-loaders, track hoes, steam rollers-- all of these vehicles will reduce zombies into so much paste. A group of survivors armed with firearms mounted on a large front-loader or bulldozer should be able to cut a bloody swathe through even a large mass of zombies. It will be slow-moving death to the undead.

Unarmed Combat

We've all been in fist fights at some point. Or most of us have been. Sort of. In something that looks vaguely like two hominids trying to ineffectually squeeze and poke one another. That is, most of us suck at hand fighting. We just don't do it enough. If you do, you're either 1) a biker, 2) a convict or you were previously, 3) a cop (but that's specialized), 4) a professional boxer/wrestler, 5) a practicing martial artist. In other words, most people aren't good at fighting with bare hands. We're actually not really equipped for it, from an evolutionary point of view. Neanderthal man was, and was strong enough to rip bits off of you. But alas, the bigger muscles and smaller brain not a success story did make. That is actually a wonderful lesson regarding the utility of unarmed combat in the zombie apocalypse. Unarmed combat against zombies is foolish. Some of my fellow experts would argue otherwise, but I strenuously object. Allow me to make my case in the following pages.

People who are expert fighters (or just really mean and tough) can do a lot of damage without using any weapons. Part of this gets back to the fact that we're really not that tough. We're poorly designed to take punishment, with relatively weak muscles and dangerously exposed vital organs.

Which means if you're good at beating people up you know that the majority of the population is pretty squishy and bad in a fight. Most fights end quickly. Boxing matches are boxing matches because the people involved are trained professionals. Anyway, if you are a Shao Lin monk or a professional boxer (or whatever) you can probably take most people in a fight. The key word here is "people." Because you aren't going to be fighting people, most of the time, in the zompocalypse. Most of the people will be dead. But you will have plenty of zombies to toy with.

There are a number of glaring problems with the concept of trying to fight zombies unarmed. First, the zombies themselves. Consider, for example, that a zombie is nothing more than a sack of meat and bones that wants to eat you. It isn't really alive, but it is presumably host to a lot of little things that are---the bacteria that are hitching a ride on the slowly-rotting body of the zombie. These bacteria are dangerous, and if you start wrestling around with the zombie you're likely to come into close contact with them. These organisms don't have your best interests in mind and should be avoided. Also note that this is over and above whatever pathogen created the zombie in the first place. If you don't want to get infected it's probably a good idea to keep your hands to yourself.

Speaking of hands, notice that the typical attack utilized by the vast majority of the non-trained populace in a fist fight is, well, a fist. And the fist is not an ideal weapon. Even using one against humans is dangerous. The human mouth is more or less as dirty, bacteria-wise, as a dog's mouth is. The chance of getting a nasty and potentially dangerous infection makes this a bad idea. Before the apocalypse cutting your hands on some other dirty human's teeth wasn't too much of a problem because of antibacterial soap and antibiotics. Yet again, the problem is a lack of medical care. And punching a zombie is much worse than punching a human, because they're infected with whatever made them zombies and carrying around who knows what other bacterial hitchhikers. You don't want to punch a zombie. Ever.

Once again, zombies can only be destroyed by destroying the brain. Unless you have a handy parking tie or some other hard inanimate object to bash the zombie's head against, good luck. The skull is the hardest part of the body for a reason and you aren't going to be able to get through that with your limbs. The Shao Lin monks in the room might beg to differ, but all the regular people should never take it the street with a zombie.

Another reason why it is extremely stupid to try to go hands-on with the undead is related to the nature of the zombie brain, and how it's different than yours or mine. We, you see, (as living breathing humans) are not normally capable of exerting our muscles to their full potential. The very good reason behind this is that if we did so we would risk damaging muscles, bones and connective tissue. Our brains stop us from going fully berserk because the brain is interested in not ripping important parts that it might want to use later. The zombie, with a mushy and primitive brain, does not have this restriction. So zombies can exert their muscles to the full extent of their power. Zombies that look smaller than you will very likely be stronger. And the zombie doesn't care if it rips muscles or damages tendons. This makes unarmed combat with zombies extremely dangerous. If you can't get away, you're lunch.

For some real-world evidence to back up my assertion that you should pretty much never go unarmed against a zombie I offer you something Bruce Lee once said (and I'm paraphrasing): "if someone wants to bite your nose off, and they're willing to take whatever punishment you might inflict to make that happen, then they'll probably get the nose." This, by definition, is exactly what a zombie is like in a fist fight. They don't care at all what you do to them, they just want the nose. And the rest of the stuff attached to the nose.

More evidence about the dangers inherent in hand fighting with zombies comes from a friend of mine who is a policeman. The individual in question has a not-quite-politically-correct term for the strength displayed by many people who have mental problems. The same concept works for individuals who have been partaking of illegal substances that aren't good for them. Being really stoned or crazy can allow people to short-circuit the mechanism that normally doesn't let the body harm itself through its own strength. These people can be extremely strong, and the police are very careful when they deal with them. Zombies, in terms of strength, are going to be like the guys who get blasted on PCP and pick a fight with a dozen cops. You really don't want to take them on by your lonesome.

The only advantage you as a live human has against the undead in terms of bare-handed fighting is speed. Zombies are slow, and so if you're careful you have the ability to outmaneuver them. As long as they don't grab hold of you, you can outrun them or flank them. Zombies have relatively poor coordination, and they can be pushed or shoved in order to unbalance them or knock them over. A kick to the back of a knee should be enough to temporarily hobble your zombie opponent. A sharp enough blow or kick to the side of the knee may break it, inflicting a more permanent crippling injury to the zombie. Attacks like these are not designed to do anything other than gain you enough time to make your escape. Fighting against even one zombie without a weapon is extremely dangerous, and you should break contact as quickly as possible. Once this has been accomplished you can keep going and make good your escape and arm yourself in order to re-engage the zombie(s) on better terms. If you are caught unarmed by a group of zombies, your only hope is to break contact and escape as quickly as possible. It is not possible for unarmed and unarmored humans to survive combat with multiple zombies. In such a situation the odds are simply too stacked in favor of the undead.

Killing a zombie, in the absence of weapons, is a difficult task. If you are able to grab the zombie's head and twist it sideways violently enough you may be able to sever the spinal cord, which would deactivate the zombie from the neck down. The zombie's jaws would remain dangerous, but it would be incapable of locomotion. In order to do this, you will have to be extremely careful to avoid the zombie's jaws prior to the snapping of its neck—just because you've grabbed the zombie by the head doesn't mean that it will desist from its primary and only motivation, which is eating you. Action movies have done a good job of making it seem relatively easy to break someone's neck with a quick twisting motion. In reality this is more difficult than the movies make it seem, in part because the person in question is going to be resisting your attempts. In terms of the zombie, the muscles of the neck will almost certainly be tensed as it continues its single-minded assault on your person. With a wriggling (and very strong) zombie trying fanatically to chew on your flesh it's going to be more difficult to emulate Hollywood's action stars than you think.

There are two relatively basic street fighting techniques that you might be tempted to use against zombies. Pitted against a human opponent these things are extremely deadly, pretty much assured to stop a fight, even if they don't kill outright. The first is gouging an opponent's eyes with the thumbs or one or both hands. The second involves violently thrusting an opponent's head sideways while simultaneously driving your knee into the relatively soft portion of the skull around the ears. Both of these things work against people, although they take a simple brawl and elevate it into the realm of attempted murder. But then in the zompocalypse there is no such thing.

So. Eye gouging. This is a particularly gruesome and terrifying wound to inflict upon a human opponent. The eyes are filled with fluid which is somewhat pressurized. If even a small pin is thrust far enough into the eye this fluid will leak out, and blindness is certain. Eyes can be crushed and burst open by the strength of the hands, if you have the fortitude to actually delve into an opponent's head. Beyond the eyes are the relatively weak bones of the ocular cavities. Humans can be killed with a determined enough assault on the eye sockets. Even if this doesn't kill the effect of losing one or both eyes may be so traumatic that you will have brought an end to a fight. Against zombies, this is not so effective.

As usual, there is no psychological impact on a zombie when you pop one or both of its eyes. They don't feel pain and lack the ability to anticipate a future of partial or total blindness. They simply don't care at all. Moreover, in order to attack the eyes you're placing yourself into the potentially very strong embrace of the zombie to your front, with what will probably be disastrous consequences. If you have the physical strength necessary to fight off the zombie while you continue your assault on its eyes, keep in mind that putting your fingers into the insides of a zombie's skull is a very good way to get infected, or at least get a very dangerous "normal" bacterial infection that could also kill you. Delving around in a zombie's body, especially while it's fully animated, should clearly be avoided at all costs.

Smashing the side of an opponent's skull is a potentially lethal attack on a human. The skull is weak at the side of head, and is much less able to stop intrusive attacks. Against a human, driving a knee into this relatively soft part of the skull is a good way to inflict a serious brain injury. With a hard enough blow the brain will swell, resulting in unconsciousness and death. As above, you've probably gone into the territory of attempted murder. But, zombies, as usual, don't cooperate.

A zombie's brain is only partially functional, so there's no guarantee that you'll be able to inflict enough damage to put your zombie down by battering it with a knee or elbow. While you're attempting to knock your way through its skull, the zombie will still be trying to grab and bite. In order to knee the zombie in the head in the first place, you'll also need to push its head downwards towards your rising knee—an activity that is dangerous in several different respects. Grabbing the side of the zombie's head may result in a bite. Pushing the zombie's head into your knee may also result in a bite. And since bites are fatal, you've just lost in a very final way.

As I conclude this section I would like to reiterate that unarmed hand-to-hand combat against zombies is extremely dangerous. It is something to be avoided unless you have absolutely no choice at all. It would be better to run. The dangers of fighting a zombie unarmed put it just to one side of being suicidal. Even fully trained professional fighters (boxers, etc.) are going to notice that their skills, which worked so well against living humans, are more than trumped by the vast advantages zombies enjoy in an unarmed encounter at arm's length. This is not to say that contemplating unarmed combat is bad. As with everything else in this volume survival is a prize won by those who are the most adaptable to changing conditions. In Darwinian terms, survivors who are willing to use every tool and every technique are those survivors whose survival is "selected for." So unarmed combat should not entirely be stricken from your zompocalypse playbook. But if flight or armed combat are options these should always be chosen first. Hand fighting is the last resort of the desperate.

Know your limits

The last word on close combat, whether armed or unarmed, has to revolve around a realistic self-assessment of your physical and mental capabilities. For many of us the closest we've ever been to lethal combat is in the seats of movie theater or perched in front of a computer monitor or TV screen. Some individuals have slaughtered untold thousands of simulated human and inhuman enemies in the artificial realm of video game worlds. But very few of us have actually needed to fight desperately to survive. This is a serious liability, and careful thought is required on the part of each and every zompocalypse survivor to overcome this handicap.

For starters, movies and video games make fighting and killing look deceptively easy and painless. The psychological issues which make real warfare so traumatizing are absent. The physical pain of wounds and the fear of being wounded are removed. In short, these are deceptive images of violence, and a realistic real-world contemplation of what combat entails is something that is valuable to all survivors.

First off, you should thoroughly analyze your physical abilities, especially as they pertain to moving and jumping. In the zompocalypse you will be forever outnumbered, and the need to escape will be more or less constantly hovering in the background. Running, climbing, jumping and crawling are the means through which you will live to fight another day, and so you need to know very closely how able you are to accomplish these things. It doesn't necessarily matter if you aren't an Olympic-level athlete as long as you know your personal limitations. If you can't run fast, you should factor that into your plans. If you don't have enough upper-body strength to climb well, then make sure you don't back yourself into a corner where the only way out is up. There is no one correct answer or perfect solution to ensure survival. Instead, staying alive is dependent upon you knowing what you are and aren't capable of and acting accordingly.

In battle you will be constrained by the limitations of your muscular strength and endurance. Exertion and adrenaline will combine to tire you out, especially if you're fighting with a hand weapon. For every encounter there is a sort of internal clock that you need to pay attention to. It is of the utmost importance to always save enough energy to get away. Keeping multiple escape routes open is an excellent idea, but they won't do you any good if you tire yourself out so severely as to hamper your escape. Discretion is always the better part of valor in zombie warfare.

Knowing your limits also pertains to firearms or other ranged weaponry. If you're using a gun or a bow you need to engage the enemy only up to the point where you have sufficient ammunition to stay in the fight. An empty gun or bow is worthless dead weight. Remember that survival is best ensured by fighting as much as possible on your own terms. If you can defeat your opponents with minimal risk to yourself or members of your group, engage. If not, hide or flee. There is no glory in being ripped apart by a horde of zombies you had no hope of overcoming.

Despite what movies and video games might suggest, under the stress of combat most people don't shoot very accurately. This is why in police gunfights dozens of bullets might be fired and the offending perpetrator is struck only a handful of times. Stress does funny things to fine motor skills. Zombies are all least relatively slow targets that won't dodge or take cover, but you should not anticipate hitting the bull's eye with every shot. Depending on skill level, you might miss quite a bit. Your target area on a zombie is rather small, after all.

Your physical limitations also need to be calculated according to the available nutrition and your overall state of health. If you're sick or malnourished you should not count on being very effective for very long in close combat. This is even more so if you're counting on using a heavy edged or blunt weapon of any kind or if you're encumbered by armor or equipment. Note that in ancient warfare battles included numerous small pauses during their course—humans are simply not physically capable of fighting for hours on end without rest. Ten or fifteen minutes of combat with a sword or axe is going to feel like an eternity, and you'll be exhausted afterwards. If you want to look to a modern example of this at work look up any professional boxing match on the internet and note the exhaustion of the two fighters. There is a reason why the fights are broken into rounds with short pauses for rest. And professional boxers are normally in extraordinarily good shape, having trained relentlessly for the short periods where they'll be in the ring. If they get worn out in a fight, you should expect that you won't be doing as well. Probably not even close.

If this discussion concerns you one of the most productive things you can do is learn to be more active. Go to the gym. Take up jogging. Go for regular walks. Anything that increases your physical health prior to the zompocalypse is a good thing. The better shape you're in, the more likely you are to survive. Your immune system will be stronger, resulting in less chance of you catching a cold that might compromise your ability to fight or flee. Muscles that are already prepared to run, move and lift will be better allies as you escape the hordes, or turn to fight back. The zompocalypse will not be kind to many modern-day couch potatoes who spend too much time eating too much of the wrong kinds of food. All they're really doing is turning themselves into food—and it will be the undead who do the eating. Do yourself a favor and don't belong to this group of future zombie snack foods.

Defensive Weapons: Armor

Warfare in the ancient world, or the later medieval periods of Europe, Asia and Africa revolved around the use of offensive and defensive weaponry. Offensive weapons in a variety of forms have already been covered at length. Any discussion of warfare that omits defensive measures is incomplete, however, because no offense is really effective without complementary defenses. The ability to inflict damage on other humans is a key part of warfare, but without the ability to deflect, absorb or redirect the attacks of your opponents your life as a warrior will be short. The following discussion offers a brief overview of the history of armor, and leads into an analysis of the utility of armor in the specialized warzones of the zombie apocalypse.

Even the very earliest warriors wore armor, or that is they wore items that protected them in the same way that later armors would. Clothing made of animal skins or woven from plant or animal fibers is fully capable of proving defensive protection in a fight. Human combatants need this very badly, because we're more or less squishy sacks of meat with exposed vital organs. Anything that keeps weapons from piercing or bashing our soft bodies is a good thing if you plan on getting in a fight against weapon-bearing enemies.

Warfare really took off with the beginning of agriculture, which also saw an associated explosion of various material technologies that could be applied to warfare. The technology of metal weaponry, both bronze and iron, made warfare more deadly than before. In response to this the warriors of the ancient Near East developed various kinds of defensive countermeasures to help ensure that they could inflict damage on the battlefield and live to fight on another one later on. Their solution was body armor and the defensive weapons we call shields.

The earliest purpose-built body armor was predominately made of natural materials, since these were cheaper and lighter than metal. Egyptian depictions of warfare show Egyptian warriors wearing armor that was probably constructed of quilted cloth, with helmets of similar design. They also bore shields, probably of ox-hide and wood, and their various opponents were similarly equipped. Warriors in the ancient Near East wore helmets of various materials and designs. These might even be made of bronze, which was expensive but resilient. And as you know, nature has designed you with a mind to protecting the contents of your skull.

Treated hides or quilted cloth made effective armor, probably more so than most people think. Metal armor was flashy, a sign of wealth. It did provide good protection. But it was also extremely expensive, very heavy and often unbearably hot to wear in the sun. The Greeks, famous for a particular kind of bronze armor, actually abandoned bronze, more or less, for anything other than the helmet. Their replacement equipment was body armor made from layers of linen cloth, glued together and perhaps reinforced at strategic areas by leather or bronze scales. These cuirasses were much lighter, less expensive, and less prone to causing the wearer to suffer heat stroke. In the warfare of the Spanish conquest of the Aztec Empire in the early sixteenth century much is often made of the technological disparity between the Aztecs and the Spanish conquistadores. What is not usually noted is that by the end of Aztec resistance most of the Spanish soldiers had replaced their heavy, stifling metal armor for cloth protection similar to what the Aztecs themselves used. Indeed, cloth armors (and various kinds of leather armor) were used alongside metal armor throughout the entirety of the European Middle Ages. These were cheap and reasonably effective and they didn't tire out the wearer as much as metal protection did. The rise of full articulated plate armor late in the medieval period actually saw a resurgence in the use of cloth and leather protections for most soldiers. The knight in full plate armor was wearing (for the time) an enormously expensive system of passive defense, and most warriors couldn't afford to follow suit. So they opted for the greater mobility provided by cloth or leather armor. After all, the fully armored knight couldn't move as fast as more lightly armored opponent, and so this provided at least of hope of avoiding attacks while remaining partially protected. This is the reason that late-medieval European knights carried a variety of weapons---some were armor-piercing, meant to deal with their fellow nobles, while other tools were carried to take down more lightly armored soldiers, who were more numerous on the battlefield.

In Asia armor followed more or less the same path as in Europe, although it never developed into the full plate armor that appeared in Europe shortly before advances in gunpowder weaponry made armor obsolete there. In China and Japan armor was usually based around composite construction techniques that used leather or metal scales and plates to reinforce a cloth or leather backing. Mail was used in China and Japan, with minor differences in construction from the patterns used in Europe. In Japan warriors developed a particularly beautiful type of armor that utilized silk cords and leather/metal scales. The resulting body armor was flexible and relatively light, and the use of silk allowed it to be very effective against arrows or slashing weapons. Thrusts could find their way through, as in Europe, especially if they hit the right spot. But overall the armor was light and quite effective at keeping its wearer alive.

Both in Europe and Asia body armor declined with the development of more effective firearms. For a time there was an arms race between armorers and gun makers, which led to heavier suits of armor meant to stop musket balls. By the end of the sixteenth century this race had more or less been definitely won by the gun manufacturers. There was simply a limit beyond which metal, leather and silk could no longer keep the bullets out. Once it became clear that even the finest (and most expensive) armor could be pierced by bullets, armor and the practice of wearing it began to go into decline. Specialized armors managed to stick around, even for centuries after guns had won the contest. In Poland the famous "Winged Hussars," a type of heavy cavalry, continued to wear expensive shot-proof armor into the seventeenth and eighteenth centuries. Their heavy panoplies included articulated breastplates, helmets and vambraces (forearm guards) that could repel pistol bullets at point-blank range, and musket balls from somewhat farther out. But a musket shot at close range, where muskets were really effective, would go straight through into the man behind the metal. By the Napoleonic period only very specialized heavy cavalry wore substantial metal body armor: the cuirassiers, who were the last descendants of medieval knights. They wore extremely heavy breastplates that could turn pistol balls up close and musket shot from medium range, as well as steel helmets. Their equipment made them formidable opponents in hand to hand combat with other cavalry. Against infantry their appearance was enough to scare their opponents, but musket balls went through the armor, as Wellington's infantry found when they surveyed the battlefield after the battle of Waterloo in 1815.

For a time body armor was absent from the battlefield. From the later part of the nineteenth century through World War Two there wasn't much use for body armor because material technology couldn't defeat the offensive power of high velocity bullets. But even in this dry spell some armor found a use. In World War One specialized metal armor was used in small amounts by some troops amid the stalemate of trench warfare. The widespread re-adoption of metal helmets by most of the belligerent forces in that war saved large numbers of soldiers from shell splinters. But beyond the utility of metal helmets body armor couldn't really do much against heavy artillery or .30 caliber rifle and machinegun bullets.

Another rather specialized appearance of body armor came in the wake of the Great Depression. The economic collapse saw a rising crime wave propelled by professional armed robbers like John Dillenger. Many of these criminals used military-grade weaponry, and so they could usually outgun the police forces intended to stop them. One of the tricks up the sleeves of Depression-era thieves was a form of body armor that was of great antiquity, and which was actually pretty effective. Thickly padded cotton body armors worn under clothing could and did stop most low velocity pistol rounds, even at close range. The .38 caliber revolvers used by most policemen could be defeated by these vests, and so the robbers had even more of an advantage against their outgunned opponents. The development of the .357 Magnum cartridge was partially due to the failure of the .38 Special against this type of armor—the velocity of the new round was high enough to penetrate armor, and the engine blocks of getaway vehicles for that matter.

There was some attempt to apply silk technology to bullet-resistant body armors, but the expense of the fibers was and is prohibitive. The creation of the synthetic fiber Kevlar in the twentieth century led to a comeback for body armor, which is now routinely worn by the soldiers of wealthy armies and police in the course of their duties. Kevlar armor supplemented by ceramic plates of a special design can even defeat rifle bullets. The best armors tend to be quite heavy, and are relatively uncomfortable and hot, but they do save lives. The weight of these modern armors more or less inhibits their use in the zompocalypse, but zombies don't use guns, so you won't have too much need for heavy military-grade body armor.

So. The above short history introduced body armor and gave you some account of the scope and history of its use by warriors in battle. How does this description of the history of armor relate to a discussion of zombie warfare and battle tactics? In a number of ways, actually.

Most body armors throughout history were at least partially designed to deflect or absorb the impact of missile weapons. They were quite good in this role. Even the cloth armor used by the Greeks in the fifth century BCE could pretty much stop arrows unless they were fired at extremely close range. This quality of body armor is only of marginal importance against zombies, because they are by their nature specialized hand-to-hand combatants, a type of slow-moving shock infantry if you will. But armor's ability to defeat cutting attacks, in this case the bite of a zombie or the raking of possible exposed bones on the hands, is something that merits your close attention.

You won't be using full plate armor, as in the style of late medieval Europe. Wearing a full suit of plate would protect you quite well from the zombies, but would also be heavy and tiring and eventually the undead would catch up to you and start to pile up. Eventually you'd be trapped in your metal skin by the press of zombies and succumb either to persistent chewing or dehydration. But European plate armor isn't going to be commonly encountered by the average apocalyptic survivor. The armor you will come across most commonly are the riot armors and bullet-resistant vests used by law enforcement and military personnel.

These armors are not without their uses against zombies. For example, the PASGT vest, which is the basis for US military body armor, is actually quite a useful piece of equipment, should you encounter one. They aren't weightless—they tip the scales at around nine pounds, but there is a payoff for the extra weight. A PASGT vest has articulation in the back and at the shoulders, and protects the neck and torso from bites. It also has layered Kevlar designed to defeat most things up to and including .44 Remington magnum. It isn't proof against rifle rounds, but shrapnel, shotgun pellets, handgun bullets and zombie teeth won't get through it. It also has magazine pouches and attachment points. Plus you'll look (and feel) hard-core. Always a good thing.

As with offensive weaponry, it is important to consider things that aren't meant to be armor but that will serve that purpose in a pinch. Also of potential importance is your ability to construct armor or reinforce items of clothing to serve as protective garments. Similarly to the issue with weaponry, the best survivors are the innovative ones.

Before you think about what types of protective clothing you might scavenge or construct, you should consider the main weapons of the zombie and the most likely targets for these weapons. Zombies aren't selective—they come straight at you and try to bite the first thing they encounter. Which means, given the proximity of their teeth to your body, some of your bits are more likely to be attacked and therefore more deserving of being armored. A standing zombie is most likely to bite offensively to a human's neck and shoulders. Arms are likely targets because they will instinctively be used to defend against incoming attacks. The face is also vulnerable, but again the instinctive reaction of most people will be to turn the face and head away and block with the arms and hands. So if you're looking to reach a happy medium between carried weight and efficient protection, you should be looking for a way to armor your hands, forearms, shoulders and neck. The PASGT vest, mentioned above, will serve for everything except the arms and hands, so it's a useful find for a lucky scavenger. But you aren't limited to purpose-built military armor, in part due to the limitations of the zombie's principal means of attack.

As in other areas of zombie capabilities, the bite of a zombie is somewhat superhuman but ultimately limited by the fact they share our underlying biology. While the zombie can bite harder than you can—a zombie doesn't care about damage to the teeth or the musculature that supports the jaws—they still have the same essentially weak jaw that you do. Human jaws are multipurpose structures capable of grinding hard plant foods and chewing meat. But they aren't specialized to cut through and tear up flesh, as are the jaws of lions or housecats. Humans, moreover, learned a long time ago to use fire (and other means) to process food to make it easier to chew. We just don't have very powerful jaws. While we can inflict bite wounds, we're nowhere near as impressive as something like, say, a Rottweiler. What all this means is that it shouldn't take very much armor to provide at least short-term protection from the bites of hungry zombies.

A heavy leather jacket, if the climate allows you to wear one, should provide decent protection from zombie bites. You don't want to stop and let them chew on you at length, but the zombie that you don't see who manages to get close and take a taste of your left shoulder won't get through the jacket in one bite. Instead, it will get a mouthful of treated leather that will stop its teeth from reaching your vulnerable skin. Clothing will perform the same task, as long as you're wearing enough layers.

Outside the realm of pre-made garments or body armor is where things start to get interesting. Consider, for example, that mail (erroneously called "chain mail" in popular culture, when the appropriate term is "mail" or "maille") armor was used by European and other warriors for most of two millennia to stop arrows and cutting weapons. And while mail armor is not going to be a common find of your scavenging expeditions, it is relatively easy (but time consuming) to make. The standard European pattern of four rings through a central fifth ring is very easy to make, and rings can be constructed with minimal tools. If you have a large nail, metal rod, or even a pen (not pencils, they're too soft) you can wind wire to form a spring-like cylinder of rings. With some wire cutters these become open individual rings, and a pair of pliers and some patience will do the rest. Bits of mail can be sown to preexisting garments as reinforcement. You're not looking to make a full-length mail shirt, just enough to protect your most vulnerable parts.

Leather can be used in a variety of ways to provide reasonably bite-proof armor pieces. Any old pair of cowboy boots (surprisingly common at thrift stores) can be quickly made into vambraces, meant to protect the forearms. These can be made with just a knife, with any handy thread, cord or shoelace pressed into service to bind them to your arms. Simply cut away the leather upper from the soles and then slit the resulting tube lengthwise. This will leave you with a curled and roughly rectangular piece of heavy leather. Bore holes for your bindings with the point of your knife. The size can be adjusted to your anatomy beforehand by trimming the leather. You'll get extra style points by using excess leather to cut a rounded square to cover the back of your hand up to your knuckles. Once this is laced to the protection on your forearm you have an effective shield that zombies won't be able to bite through. If you're nervous this protection can be easily reinforced further with mail or the application of washers or other metal supports. Sewing small washers (from any hardware store) to your leather vambraces will give you a sort of armor Europeans sometimes called "ring armor" or "ring mail." Since you've got time on your hands, there is really no excuse for wandering around the zompocalypse dressed only in a t-shirt. Remember, everybody is a warrior in the zombie world. You have no choice. And warriors don't go to battle against superior numbers without thinking about adequate offense and defense. A savvy partially-armored survivor is going to greatly increase his or her survivability in close combat with the undead. As soon as you can, find some way to protect the areas of your body most vulnerable to zombie attack.

Shields are your Friends

In the ancient wars of the Fertile Crescent and the conflicts between Egypt and the Hittite lords of Anatolia (modern-day Turkey), shields were probably the most important single defensive measure available. Most of the armor available in the Bronze Age was light weight and covered the body only sparsely. Shields were cheap, effective, and available. Most warriors would have carried one, and those who didn't were defended by others who did.

Throughout classical antiquity shields were carried by pretty much all of the warriors of the Greco-Roman Mediterranean. A few of them even became famous, or at least as famous as a type of shield can be in a society that now knows iPads and e-readers and solar power generation. The shield used by the Greek hoplites who fought at Marathon and Plataea (490 and 479 BCE) is one of these, often erroneously called a "hoplon." A more accurate term is "aspis," since the word "hopla" refers to armament in a more general sense. The hoplite was simply a (fully) armed and armored man. Anyway, the shield used by ancient Greek hoplites was beautiful and effective, as well as being expensive and technologically complex. Roughly three feet in diameter, it was composed of a bowl-shaped wooden core covered over with an outer facing of bronze. Held by a handgrip and secured around the forearm such a shield could stop even determined spear thrusts, let alone arrows and sling bullets. Offensively, the shield could be used to inflict a blow with its edge more than sufficient to crush a man's skull.

Later the Roman legionaries of the Republic (and most of the Principate and Dominate periods, until the decline of the Western Empire from the fourth century onwards) carried large body shields, or *scuta* (sg. *scutum*). These were held with a central hand grip which was protected by a bronze hand guard called an *umbo*. Such shields would ward off missiles of all kinds and formed a mobile barricade that protected the legionaries in close combat. You could stab your short sword out from behind the shield and inflict a wound, and then quickly recover it and go back to a guard position behind the shield. Used in the fighting formations of the legions these two tools were morbidly effective.

Shields were used by warriors of all classes throughout most of the medieval period, though their use declined in the fifteenth century. The reason for this decline was that armor had become heavier and more effective until even many poor foot soldiers were equipped with at least partial plate armor. An arm encased in articulated plates was fairly impervious to most weapons, meaning that a warrior could ward off attacks or grapple with his left arm and wield a sword or axe or mace in his right. The extra free hand also allowed the use of polearms like halberds and glaives, which were effective weapons even against armor. Social elites, of course, benefited from expensive suits of full plate armor, making them walking tanks on the battlefield. Shields were still used by some, but the advance of armor technology started to make them obsolete.

It wasn't long before the increasing effectiveness of firearms also "did for" the armor itself. Once bullets routinely began to pierce through the expensive stuff, warriors started to dress lighter and lighter until armor was replaced by military uniforms. Eventually pretty much everyone was carrying around firearms and armor was restricted to specialized heavy cavalry or represented by the vestigial and symbolic—the metal gorgets worn by eighteenth century infantry officers are an example of this practice at work.

The shield has not completely disappeared from use, despite the massive leaps in military technology that have occurred since people started abandoning them in the fifteenth century. If you've ever been part of a riot or demonstration and the police showed up, then you know what I'm talking about. In law enforcement circles shields are still a part of the tool set, used by riot police and in a specialized form by SWAT officers. It is the first of these uses that is the most intriguing from your point of view as a survivor of the apocalypse.

Used against crowds (note: I personally consider the use of riot police against crowds of protestors to be a infringement of free speech, in many cases...we're talking about the use of shields against zombies, just let me get to it), policemen and women armed with polymer shields protect themselves from thrown projectiles by interposing their shields. Such shields are also used to block and push people back and herd them into tight spaces. Police generally aren't going to use shields like a medieval or ancient warrior might, i.e. as a bludgeoning weapon capable of inflicting a mortal wound. They're generally more passive, given that killing protestors carries legal ramifications. But shields they have, and they definitely use them.

If you happen to find one of these transparent police riot shields (remember the breakdown of civilization?) it might be a useful addition to your pile of swag. This is especially true if you've followed the advice above and have a secure base to store some additional items. Such shields are made to take a lot of punishment, at least from unarmed human bodies, and should last a long time. They would prove to be quite effective at keeping zombies away from your soft bits, near enough for you to strike them but incapable of inflicting their own wounds. They aren't particularly heavy, which is good in the sense that the weight savings makes them more practical for weight-conscious survivors to consider carrying. The light weight is bad in the sense that it makes them much less viable as weapons, which was one of the benefits of ancient shields. If you don't believe me then consider the following—the Romans have at least one historical anecdote that I can think of where a Roman soldier lost his hand or arm to a sword and managed to kill his opponent with nothing but a shield. Manly, no?

If you really want to inflict some carnage of your own (on the undead at least...shields don't stop bullets) you'll need to put on your creative thinking cap. Riot shields are meant to stop, block and push, not to crush. You'll need something more specialized if you shield is to be a supplementary weapon in its own right. This takes you back to the handy dandy home improvement store, where all good things are to be found.

Some late medieval shields were made of steel, but they were late anomalies in the history of shield design. Nearly all shields were made out of organic materials, principally wood, leather and cloth. Many shields, such as those used by the Romans, were made of plywood. Thin strips of wood would be laced together, overlapped and glued into a solid piece. Shields would be steamed in a special mold to form them into a curved shape, but that takes special technology and makes your task more difficult.

If I needed to make a usable shield in a hurry from materials on hand, I would find my inspiration in the flat round shields used by Viking and Anglo-Saxon warriors in the early Middle Ages. These varied in size up to three feet in diameter and were between a quarter and a half-inch thick, made from glued boards. The outer faces of shields were often covered with cloth or hide, also attached by glue. The facing material helped to prevent splintering and cracking and made the whole structure stronger. The edges of shields were reinforced by leather or metal, meant like the facing material to extend the life of the shield and prevent catastrophic damage. You probably won't find specially forged metal reinforcements at your home improvement store, but a bit of ingenuity will solve this (and any) problem. Grab yourself some of the big leathery dog bones from petty much any supermarket—an unlikely item for looters—and you've found yourself usable rawhide. Soak these bones in water and unravel them and you have lengths of rawhide to reinforce your shield. Once they are cut, stretched and tacked onto your shield rim all you have to do is wait for them to dry. Once they've dried hard your shield will be quite strong, capable even of medieval combat. Add a handgrip—the Greek-style configuration, with a grip near the shield's rim and a loop for the forearm behind it is probably the best idea—and you're ready for battle.

In close combat with zombies a shield is an excellent friend to have. Shields can and should be used to block the dangerous bits of the zombie (the teeth) while you strike from behind the shield with a hand weapon (or even a pistol or revolver). Like the Romans and other warriors who used shields, you'll be relatively free to strike at exposed flesh, even as you stay more or less safe behind your shield. If for some reason you're having a hard time striking to the zombie's skull, all you have to do is launch a crippling blow to the exposed left leg, or reach around to sever the connective tissue at the back of the knee. All you need to do at that point is apply a little force on your shield and the zombie should topple over, less mobile than before. Crippling, if done correctly, is an excellent way to thin out a group of zombies. Just watch your feet.

Always remember, if you're using a proper shield (not a polymer riot shield), that they were meant to be used offensively and were not relegated to a purely defensive role. If you've a shield in your off hand what you've really got is two weapons— the shield and whatever you're using in the other hand. Blows can be struck with either the face or the rim of a shield, and these can be quite powerful. If you've got a shield with two straps, lashed to your forearm (as opposed to having only a single central grip) you'll be able to strike very powerful blows at close range. Put your shoulder into the shield as you strike, punching outward and upward with your elbow. The force generated by such a strike is capable of killing a living human several times over. Against the slightly rotted skull of a zombie you should be able to crack into the soft stuff at the center of the tootsi...ah, well, you get the idea.

Fortification

The idea of using stone, earth, brick or wood to defend yourself against enemies is an ancient one. In fact, it predates written history. Very, very soon after human societies learned to settle and plant they found out that other groups of humans might find it easier to take what they had instead of making or growing it for themselves. The ancient peoples of the Mediterranean basin very quickly learned that if they constructed walls and watch towers they would 1) be able to learn about attacks before enemy groups arrived and 2) be able to better resist them once they got there.

The more war-torn a particular region was the more likely the people there developed the technology of forts and walls. Mycenaean Greece (c. 1200 BCE) was broken up (as one example) into a myriad of little kingdoms all fighting to keep and control the limited arable land that lay between the mountain peaks. These little kingdoms used fortifications of stone to help ensure that attacking enemies couldn't win easy, overwhelming victories.

People figured out pretty early that control of fortified places was a key component of political and economic dominance. The Assyrian Empire was one state that was quite skilled in this regard, using fortified places to defend against enemies as well as launch attacks of its own.

Fortifications were only as good as the technology to defeat them allowed them to be. In some cases this meant that fortified towns or purpose-built forts were impregnable to attack. The magnificent Spartan army, fighting the Athenians in the fifth century BCE, was completely stymied for years against the walls of Athens, which really weren't that formidable. The Spartans simply lacked the engineering ability (and the cultural predisposition) to be able to overcome stone walls. They wanted their enemies to come out and fight, which the Athenians prudently refused to do.

This changed radically during the fourth century BCE. New engineering techniques aided the aggressive kingdom of Macedon in developing an army that was supreme not only on the field of battle but in sieges as well. After a troublesome rebellion, Alexander VII (later "Megas Alexandros" or Alexander the Great) razed the ancient city of Thebes to the ground. No longer were fortified places safe from assault. In his subsequent war against the Persian Empire Alexander employed every trick and stratagem provided by what was then cutting-edge science. The siege of the city of Tyre was particularly noteworthy, in that Tyre was built on an offshore island and had walls that were two hundred feet above the surf, in some places. Alexander's army constructed a massive siege ramp extending out into the sea, in order to reach the city. Once they got there they employed siege towers (both on the ramp and mounted on pairs of ships) as well as powerful torsion catapults to assault the walls of Tyre. When they took the city the fall was accompanied by great bloodshed, with no mercy extended to the populace of that unhappy place.

During the European Middle Ages sieges were very common, and field battles were rare. In part this was due to the limitations of feudal states in regards to financing and supplying their armed forces, but a lot of it was due to the ubiquity of forts and castles. Castles served as strongpoints that couldn't be left behind due to the danger they presented to an army's lines of communication and supply. Even the small garrisons that most castles had could wreck havoc if they were bypassed and nobody was left to watch them. So an army encountering a castle had to lay siege to it. The problem then was that sieges took a very long time, and money often ran out before the castle fell. Most medieval warfare was characterized by a lack of results, due to the number of castles that dotted the landscape. Wars were limited to a few sieges that decided little, and large conquests of territory were as rare as major field battles.

A good example of the effectiveness of castles in controlling a population and providing for defense in a hostile territory can be found in the eleventh century Norman invasion of Anglo-Saxon England. The Saxons had few fortifications, preferring to rely upon professional warriors backed up by a citizen militia for defense. When the Normans won the Battle of Hastings in the fall of 1066, they almost immediately started to construct timber forts and castles throughout the country. Rebels couldn't take fortified places easily, and the garrisons were on hand to counterattack. The spread of castles throughout Europe was directly related to the control of territory. When Europe's kings grew more powerful by the later Middle Ages, they restricted the number and location of fortresses, because without them rebellion was much more difficult.

The entire history of fortifications and fortresses is a vast subject, and I won't go into detail about the later evolution of fortifications, in part because they were designed to serve against dangers you won't be facing in a zombie apocalypse. Zombies don't have artillery. But the short history I've already supplied above has some very important lessons embedded within it for zompocalypse survivors.

Take, for the example, the medieval castle. In their mature form (such as Krak des Chevaliers, or "Castle of the Knights," in what is modern-day Syria), these fortresses were capable of tying up large numbers of enemy troops with a minimum commitment of one's own forces. The castle was operated for a time by the Knights Hospitaller, and as with all crusader forces in the Middle East manpower was always at a premium. The Knight-brothers who manned Les Krak des Chevaliers were lucky to defend a fortress that had been masterfully built to allow effective defense with a minimal number of defenders.

Good castles had a number of basic features that should apply, ideally, to all apocalyptic fortresses. They, of course, were tough enough to resist attack by the weapons (mostly various kinds of catapult) that might be brought against them. Beyond this, a number of important design features made European (and non-European) castles able to resist attack and serve as a base of assault for their occupants. First, the number of entrances needed to be limited, because they were a focus of enemy attacks. What entrances there were needed to be reinforced so that they couldn't be forced open. Second, there needed to be a supply of food and water so that the garrison could survive a lengthy siege. Third, there needed to be sally ports so that defenders could make surprise attacks on enemy forces or flee if the fortress was breached. Fourth, a castle needed an armory of weapons to equip the forces stationed inside, and there needed to be firing ports and positions to direct fire upon surrounding enemies. Where possible, defenses were always found in depth, so that taking one part of a fortress exposed enemies to fire from another part of it. Redundant defenses meant the people inside could hold out longer, and the longer they lasted the more likely it was that they would be relieved by allied forces or their enemies would run out of money or supplies and go home. All of these things can be provided for in a post-apocalyptic fortress, and they will make the individual or the group much better able to survive in the long run.

So what is a fortress in the zompocalypse? Any structure that can be adapted to defend you or your group against zombies, the primary threat of the zombie apocalypse. Secondarily, a fortress should be able to help protect you against human bandits, but these are two different subjects, and we'll get to the later one below. Since zombies are mostly what you'll be needing your fortress for, we'll start with them and discuss how fortified places will protect you and yours from the gnashing teeth of the undead.

Any good fortress needs to withstand the weapons used by those you might try to get inside it. In the case of zombies the list is a pretty short one, since their only weapons are their bodies. Zombies can physically assault a structure with their limbs, which means that anything that is reinforced will keep them out. Even a normal stick-built house will keep considerable numbers of zombies at bay, if certain precautions are taken. Windows are obviously a liability, since zombies can and will break through them. If you're fortifying a house, the first thing you need to do is find some way to bar or board up the windows. How effective this is depends on how sturdily you barricade them. With only light boards zombies may still be able to batter their way through, so prepare with as much care as you have time and resources for. Ideally, a fortified house should have ground-floor windows bricked over, or protected with iron bars. The initial choice of which particular space to occupy and fortify is an important one, made easier by the fact that most people are dead and most places are empty.

If you're worried, sensibly enough, about having windows secured against the dead then choose something that is already fortified or that will accept modification/improvement without too much trouble. Many houses already have their doors and windows barred over to deter criminals from entering. These preventative measures will still be available in the apocalypse. You merely have to take up residence in the right place. So choose carefully.

As far as urban/suburban houses are concerned, you should realize that they are not all created equally. Houses constructed of heavy materials are the best, because these have a chance of better holding off a pack of zombies or the bullets that bandit gangs may be firing at you. In the American Southwest adobe construction, both new and old, is excellent at withstanding punishment. Small arms aren't going to get through it, and zombies won't be able to poke holes in it. Elsewhere brick construction is excellent, and will provide similar protection. If you're lucky enough to find a house built with rammed earth you'll have a very good fortress with only minor modifications, since rammed earth has a long history of being used in walls and other defensive structures in places like China.

If a house is sturdy, the first step is reinforce the vulnerable doors and windows. Windows can be barred off, bricked over, boarded, or shut up with external (or internal) debris. You'll have a problem with lighting the inside of the structure once you get rid of the ground floor windows, but you'll be a lot safer. Most external doors need to be reinforced to make them a sturdy enough barrier to repel zombies. Your local hardware store, or even nearby houses you aren't occupying, should provide the raw materials for your fortress. Deadbolts should be used where they are available. Wooden beams or iron pipes can be used to bar doors from the inside. This technology was utilized to secure the doors of medieval fortresses, so it should serve you well against the undead. In a pinch furniture can be used to bar a door, but if you have the time your preparations should be better than this.

Make sure you're not relying upon the basic locks found on many external doors. Unless you have something going deep into the frame of the door it can be forced open, and zombies are good at the type of repetitive single-minded force needed to force doors open. Dead bolts are good, bars are better. Metal security gates with a bolted door behind them are better still. Glass doors, obviously, are a terrible idea against the undead. Once they get through that, you'll have a bunch of zombies at arm's length, and be forced to fight them in close combat in an enclosed space. Avoid this situation at all costs.

When you organize a permanent or semi-permanent fortress in the zombie apocalypse, remember that escape routes are highly important. Recall the sally ports of the medieval fortresses and make sure you have alternative means of getting in and getting out of your keep. You might to need to leave in a hurry, and you should have the access points to make this happen. Again, the medieval castle is an excellent model to base your new post-apocalyptic home on—defenses need to be redundant, with several defensible locations to fall back upon. If those fail, there should be some sort of last-ditch means of making an escape. If all else fails, your last resort is to run for it. A fortress should be designed or modified in order to allow this.

Vehicles can provide one means of rapidly abandoning a fortress if the defenses are breeched. Especially good at last-minute escapes are RVs and cargo vans. These vehicles are large enough, and tall enough, so that they can be accessed from second story windows. Thus you can make a run for it and enter your escape pod from the safety of an upper floor. Too high for zombies to reach, you'll be momentarily secure, allowing you to fire up the motor and rocket off over the bodies of any zombie unlucky enough to be in your path. As with fixed dwellings, the savvy survivor will secure and armor doors and windows on an RV or other escape pod vehicle to make them more suitable for the war that you've found yourself in.

In a multi-story house stairwells need to be controlled just like doors and windows should be. The curved stairwells in many medieval castles were designed with defense in mind. People descending these circular stairwells walked downwards in a counter clockwise direction, meaning that those coming up to attack the defenders of a tower were at a disadvantage. Since nearly everybody was right-handed, walking upwards to the right meant that your sword or spear arm was restricted by the rising stairwell. Those defending against you had greater freedom to manipulate their weaponry, giving them an edge in a fight.

Like those in medieval fortresses, the staircases in your post-apocalyptic abode need to be considered as part of your defensive preparations. They can serve as choke points against zombie attackers, because only so many can climb the staircase at once. The bodies of de-animated zombies will follow the force of gravity and fall backwards on those below them, slowing them down and ultimately creating a barrier against further attack.

Stairways can be modified or reinforced to make them more effective barriers against the undead. Broken sections or obstacles situated on stairs will be difficult for zombies to negotiate, because of their limited physical dexterity. Something as simple as tying strong rope or lengths of wire or chain across a stairway can slow zombies and provide an effective choke point to thin their numbers. A mass of zombies trying to force their way through a wire barrier, unable to get around it, will be easy prey for the bullets and longer edged weapons of defending survivors.

Every good fortress should offer its defenders the option to flee or counterattack. The sally ports of medieval castles provided for such tactical flexibility, and so you should construct or adapt your structure to provide for these things as well. Ideally a sally port allows you some protection as you prepare to attack or escape. Barricades or walls or even chain link fencing that can act to slow zombies or restrict their access to the walls of a structure should be kept in mind when you plan how to utilize your fortress. Remember that zombies are not intelligent—anything that serves to funnel their movements or keep them out of a particular area allows you to anticipate the future. You have the great advantage of being able to act according to a pre-conceived plan, so make sure you take advantage of this and plot out possible defensive scenarios.

There are an entire range of possible fortresses for you to use and adapt to your needs. Civilian housing is often not particularly suited to serving as fortifications. The needs of homeowners and post-apocalyptic survivors are very different, as you know. More specialized structures are conceivably easier to fortify, given that many types of building are already designed to keep intruders out.

University campuses usually have a range of buildings that are both very heavily constructed and designed with a certain amount of security in mind. These are usually large structures that have numerous escape routes, though many have lots of vulnerable windows. But not everything on a college campus is designed for student enjoyment. Buildings associated with university infrastructure are often veritable fortresses, constructed to protect the valuable or potentially dangerous materials and equipment they contain. The University of Arizona, my alma mater, is festooned with numerous structures that would make excellent fortresses with almost no effort on the part of the potential apocalyptic tenant.

Government buildings are also excellent choices in many ways. Police stations, fire houses and other buildings linked with state and local government should usually serve as effective bases. Essentially, the sky is the limit given the availability of real estate. There is no perfect choice, but if you keep some of the above information in mind you should be fairly well prepared to find and accessorize a defendable home.

Caution should be used around certain structures, based on the likelihood of zombies to congregate due to the movements of human groups. As civilization falls apart, people won't be static—many of them will move around in a panicked attempt to escape. Highways and major roadways are likely to be jammed with the abandoned cars of fleeing civilians. Major roadways within and without cities might be similarly packed with abandoned vehicles. Many of the people who didn't attempt to outrun the apocalypse will have chosen to either barricade themselves within their homes, or to flee to supposedly more secure locations. Many shopping centers and stores are likely to have been looted. Religious buildings will have been a final location for believers attempting to find a different sort of escape or protection as civilization crumbled around them. The problem with people joining together is that such groups are large and noisy, and so they attract zombies. Anywhere people might have massed during the panic of the early stages of the apocalypse should be approached very cautiously by careful survivors. Zombies who overran and wiped out the local Wal-Mart or church will probably remain in the general vicinity, unless something comes by to distract them. Thus you'll need to try and anticipate where people would have gathered for safety, or where they decided to loot.

This is one of the reasons for seeing university campuses as excellent locations to make a post-apocalyptic home. While colleges and universities often have large populations of students and faculty, few people make their permanent homes there. As panic spread during the initial stages of the apocalypse, most students would have fled, seeking to return to their homes. Out of state students may have been unable to do this, but even they are unlikely to have remained on campus, given the lack of food and other resources. Few people are going to want to spend the end times in a classroom or dorm, so most colleges and universities will have been emptied before the final collapse of society. This works in your favor by providing a whole range of buildings (and everything they might contain) that are both empty and devoid of nearby zombies.

A range of specialized buildings/compounds are constructed from the ground up as purpose-built fortifications. These structures are either designed to keep people in or keep people out—army bases, prisons, and major utility installations. If you can access any of these they would make excellent fortresses, allowing you to sleep, rest, and work safely. Caution should be used with these structures, however, because of the potential of encountering zombies in and around them. There is also the danger that other (potentially hostile) survivors may have been drawn there first. Even like-minded survivors whose activities don't usually include murder or cannibalism are going to be trigger happy. You don't want to be on the wrong end of the "shoot first and ask questions later" formula. Remember, no medical care.

Whatever home you choose for yourself (and possible companions), whether for long or short term occupation, keep in mind the advice offered above. It is possible to construct a safe haven in the apocalypse, as long as you keep your wits about you and think your way out of the problem. The mightiest weapon you have at your disposal is your intellect. Those who think on their feet and adapt to changing conditions will be the most likely to survive.

Case Study: Canada Island

If you asked me to apply the principles of fortification and fortress construction to a specific real-world example, then I'd choose Canada Island, located on the Spokane River in my hometown of Spokane, Washington. What follows is a short explanation of the how's and why's behind my choice of Canada Island as anti-zombie fortress, and it should serve to further illustrate the points that I've set forth above.

Canada Island is only an island in a very loose sense of the word. In reality it might be more accurate to say that it is simply a large rock formation jutting out of the middle of the river, which flows to either side of the rock towards the falls immediately to the west. Canada Island is linked to the larger Riverfront Park by a road bridge that spans the river, though it isn't used for vehicles, only for foot traffic. The entirety of the park could conceivably be fortified by cutting it off from the shoreline, but the labor involved in such an endeavor would be prohibitive given the limited size of most survivor groups. Canada Island is really the better option, because of its small size.

There is actually a precedent for the island being used as a safe haven, in that both the island and the park were utilized by Spokane's early settlers to shield themselves from the wrath of the local native population. I suppose the Spokane natives weren't appreciative of groups of strange foreigners who came to steal their stuff and shoot at them. Anyway, both the park and the island would make good places to defend yourself, once you managed to shut them off from the northern and southern riverbanks.

Canada Island is connected to the land most solidly by the wide road bridge that forms its eastern boundary—besides the road bridge there are two suspended foot bridges that link the western edge of the narrow island to either shore, north and south. Other than those bridges, there is no way to reach the island, given the depth and speed of the river. Even if the river runs at unnaturally low levels, the current should be too swift to be crossed on foot, and the steep banks of the island itself form a partial cliff face. Basically, without the bridges, nobody is getting on or off the island.

The first step of anyone wanting to take up post-apocalyptic residence on Canada Island involves removing the threat of the road bridge. There are two options, as I see them, to solving this problem. The first involves explosives, and the second barricades. With option one the prospective survivor band would need to blast holes through the bridge. This would hamper the movement of human attackers and, more importantly, attacking zombies. Zombies aren't smart enough to dodge gaping holes in the floor of the bridge, you see, and so they'd come along inexorably and then inexorably plunge into the river below and be carried over the falls. If that didn't smash them to bits they'd remain animated, but the current would be sufficient to carry them down river, eventually depositing them somewhere along the lower Spokane. This would be a problem for people living down river from Canada Island, but that's, well, their problem. I'd choose a combination of gunpowder and nitrogen-based fertilizer as my explosive, though dynamite or any other available explosive would work. You would still need to employ strategic fencing with chain-link or barbed wire (or some similar barrier) in order to close gaps into your "murder holes," but this should prove effective.

A safer and more practical option (well, without the fun of playing with explosives) is to simply barricade the road bridge. I would choose a combination of city/school buses and motor homes, which would conceivably remain available as escape pods should you, need them. Fencing or walling off the remaining gaps would effectively block the road bridge to zombies, though human opponents would still remain a potential danger. With the road bridge blocked, the next step would involve dealing with the foot bridges.

These should be dealt with using the same techniques as above. Due to the narrow nature of the bridges and the constricted spaces where they both meet their respective shorelines, I would probably choose explosives and/or manual labor to cut holes in the mid-points of each bridge. Doing so shouldn't interfere too badly with the structural integrity of both structures, and a sort of drawbridge/fence could then be constructed to allow survivors from the island to block the gaps and utilize the bridges. The two bridges could also simply be gated at either end (two gates for redundant defense), though I myself would be attracted to the safety offered by the murder hole/drawbridge system. With these steps taken Canada Island should be essentially proof to even the largest zombie assault. Moreover, when positioned on the island survivors could easily direct fire in all directions, covering the shoreline and all three of the barricaded bridges.

Once secure on the island, its new tenants would be able to utilize the river as a source of fresh water, perhaps the most crucial single supply of any fortress, whether in antiquity or in the apocalypse. Further, the river could be utilized by tech-savvy individuals as a source of water-generated electricity, which a bit of leg work. The river would also be a source of fish to supplement the garrison's food supplies. Speaking of food, the nearby Riverfront Park would be a keen place to practice your farming abilities, since eventually canned foods are going to become scarce, provided you remain in one location. While you would have to get used to the white noise of the river while living on Canada Island, it would have the added benefit of cloaking any noises generated by your group, helping to shield you from the prying eyes of interested humans and hungry zombies. All in all, Canada Island would be a good choice if you needed to find a permanent or semi-permanent home in the midst of the zompocalypse.

Book II

Battle

Book I of this volume focused on weaponry—the physical items that you will use to attack and defend yourself against both human and zombie opponents. There are a great many choices, as you now know, but the primary point to take away from the preceding pages is the notion of adaptability. Being flexible in your thinking, in your fighting, in how you adapt to changing conditions—this is the true weapon of the zompocalypse survivor. Having covered weaponry and equipment above, the following sections will cover how these should best be used, both against zombies and against hostile human survivors.

Battle (as in a set piece standup fight) against groups of zombies should be considered as a legitimate subject in its own right. This goes beyond the everyday self defense that is par for the course in day-to-day encounters with the undead. It is a conscious decision to stand up to a mass of zombies and defeat them. The prizes for this include the (at least momentary) safety of yourself or your group and the spoils of war—in this case any useful items or real estate that the zombies were loitering over. Successful battle also provides crucial training for war against the undead and will serve to bolster morale, individual as well as that of any group. Obviously, failed battles deny you all this and potentially result in casualties or (if the worst happens) massacre. Clearly the subject is one that demands careful attention and thought.

The techniques of twenty-first century warfare are only of limited use on the field of battle against a force of zombies. Modern warfare uses firepower and machines and airpower to eliminate human opponents. It uses psychology and fear in combination with the material of war to annihilate an enemy or drive him in confusion from the field of battle. It dominates large swathes of territory and is related to politics and economics.

Many of these things, as you know, don't exist in the apocalypse. Against zombies the mode of war you should adopt is not that of the twenty-first century, but that of the early nineteenth, with a little bit of the medieval past mixed in. Before I go into detail about the specifics of set-piece battle against the undead, I would like to discuss the composition of a human army as it should be composed for war with the zombie horde.

The Survivor Army

The term "army" is something I (and you) should use somewhat loosely when considering the zombie apocalypse. There will simply be too few survivors to compose anything that twenty-first century people would consider an army. But, as above, adaptability and flexibility is the key to survival, and so you'll have to work with what you've got. That means that in the zompocalypse if your group is only composed of three people, then that's how big your army is. And I mean this seriously, as you'll see below.

Every good army is subdivided into specialized units that take care of different tasks. Even with your hypothetical three-human army you should consider the tasks you need fulfilled and the skill sets of members of your group. Some skills are more specialized, and more important, than others. Overall group survival is dependent upon the efficient use of the skills of each group member. Thus it is helpful to categorize members of a group of survivors according to tasks they might be most suited for.

The Scout- Good intelligence information is vital to military operations, something that has been recognized for a long time. In the Napoleonic warfare that is a useful model for anti-zombie conflicts, most intelligence information obtained "on the ground" was gathered by specialized types of light cavalry whose primary duty was scouting out the enemy. The zompocalypse scout probably won't be on horseback, but he or she might very well be on a bicycle or a scooter (some of those made by the Honda corporation are quiet enough to serve in this role). Scouting can also be done on foot, since this can be done in relative silence and zombies are not particularly fast.

A good scout's primary duty is to serve as the eyes and ears of the army behind him/her. In order to accomplish this task scouts should be men and women who are agile and fit, capable of running, jumping, and climbing. They should have good eyesight and they should supplement this with binoculars or rifle scopes so that they can spy on zombie groups or bandits from a safe distance. Scouts should be lightly armed in a way that maximizes their speed while still allowing for sustained self-defense should that be necessary. But scouts should not intend to engage the enemy by themselves. Ideally a good scout will remain unnoticed by both the living and the dead while he or she carries out his or her duties.

The ideal weapons for scouts are silenced .22 caliber rifles and pistols, weapons that allow the scout to remain silent and carry enough ammunition to survive alone for a time if they are cut off from the rest of the group. Scouts should carry a backup edged weapon like a knife, machete or short sword in order to quietly eliminate lone zombie opponents. Such weapons should really be carried by every member of every group of survivors, but the scout has more need than most of silently assassinating lone zombies.

The primary duty of a scout is the collection of information regarding enemy numbers and locations, and to a lesser extent the analysis of terrain features. When engaging zombies in full-on battle the selection of terrain is very important, and so scouts should pay attention to terrain features and buildings that might allow zombies access or restrict their movements. Communication over distance can be accomplished with hand signals and binoculars (or other sight aids) but there is no substitute for detailed reports from the scout in person. Telecommunication will be much more difficult in the apocalypse, so an army's scouts should collect information and then relay this as rapidly as possible back to the main body. Thus a scout should be in good shape and have a decent pair of shoes. Speed saves lives, both yours and those of your companions.

The Medic- The specialized knowledge of a medic makes them highly valued members of any group. I've repeatedly stressed the medieval nature of medical care once the apocalypse destroys modern civilization and the only thing that will ameliorate that is a medic of some kind. Whether the individuals are former doctors, nurses, paramedics, firemen or even people who have taken first-aid classes or volunteered in hospitals, good medics are incredibly important. This is not just because of the world-wide infestation of zombies—

there are many possible dangers to be aware of from everyday post-apocalyptic activity, so keep your medics safe. This should be taken to the extreme of keeping medics out of front-line combat as much as possible, because the death of a medic may seal the fates of other members of the group later on. Protect the priceless specialized knowledge that medics possess, because it will be hard to replace it in a world overrun by zombies.

Medics should be armed, as every group member should, with a primary weapon and a backup. In the interest of saving space and weight they should have at least a pistol and some sort of hand weapon. Whatever they're equipped with they should be capable of defending themselves and fighting if the situation requires it. As with every survivor the world of the zombie is one in which every human is a warrior. But medics are particularly valuable warriors and should be protected by other members of the group at all costs. Let other members take care of dangerous scouting or scavenging missions. It may sound cold, but the loss of general-purpose warriors is more acceptable than the loss of your only access to modern medical care.

Medical supplies for the treatment of wounds, as with everything else, will have to be manufactured or scavenged. First-aid kits and medical supplies are therefore high on the list of items to be prioritized during routine scavenging trips. At the very least a decently-equipped medic should take into the field a first-aid kit and extra clean bandages and disinfectants. Medics should be able to suture serious cuts, and should back this ability up with super-glue (not the healthiest option, but it's the apocalypse).

Other group members should carry on their persons materials to assist the medic in his or her job. All group members should at the very least have some form of clean bandage and something to disinfect a wound with. Getting an infection may be fatal in the new world, so try not to get one. Alcohol, hydrogen peroxide, soap, hand cleanser and even honey can be used to disinfect wounds, and you should not be shy about using such materials.

In terms of zombie bites it may not be possible to save a victim, but you and your group can try. If a group member is bitten and the wound has not severed major blood vessels it may be possible to use disinfectants to halt the zombie infection before it can spread. Hydrogen peroxide or alcohol, if applied rapidly enough, may allow a bite victim a chance at survival. Obviously this is a controversial issue, as other experts in the field seem to consider bites to be uniformly fatal. But swift (and brutal) application of disinfectants may offer some hope of survival. The other option, also found in the contemporary literature, is battlefield amputation. Generally speaking this should not be attempted, even if you have trained medical personnel on hand. The dangers of secondary infection and shock pretty much spell doom for your stricken comrade even without the zombie infection. Also note that you can't simply hack off a limb and expect that to serve as a medical procedure. The instruments used in such an operation should be very sharp and very sterile, and care should be taken in order not to damage nerves, bones and blood vessels any more than need be. Going medieval on your friend's leg with an axe or machete is a good way to lose your friend.

Medics, as with all group members, should be prepared for the eventuality that most victims of zombie bites or other serious wounds will not survive. The medic should assist other members of the group in dealing with wounds, but he or she should also offer aid in terms of ending the lives of those individuals who can't be saved. This is especially crucial in regards to battle, if wounded group members cannot be evacuated. Leaving someone behind to be devoured alive is a cruel fate, and suicide or mercy-killing is much preferable. Again, this may sound cold, but the apocalypse is a changed world.

The Sharpshooter- During the Napoleonic Wars armies of most nations employed some form of rifle-armed infantry for specialized tasks. In the Germanic nations these troops were called "jagers" (literally "hunters"), while the British referred to them as "Rifles" in reference to their specialized equipment. American backwoodsmen filled the same role for the colonial army during the Revolutionary War, armed with weapons that owed their origin to the German and Austrian hunters who developed them in Europe. Many of these sharpshooters, actually, carried guns made by immigrant German gunsmiths.

At any rate, sharpshooters were an important part of warfare in the age of Napoleon. Their task was specialized, and their deployment on the battlefield was designed to utilize their strengths and minimize their weaknesses. Early rifled muskets, you see, were very slow to load. The Minié bullets of the American Civil War had yet to be invented, and Napoleonic Rifles were difficult to load and fouled quickly. They were careful to stay well away from cavalry formations, and sought the protection of other infantry if enemies got too close. Their main task was to shoot enemy officers and provide harassing fire to suppress enemy troops. The long range of their weapons could be used to make sure enemy skirmishers kept their heads down, and while it was unsporting the killing of enemy officers tended to disorganize infantry formations. Ever since Napoleonic times armies have included snipers of one type or another.

In the zombie apocalypse having one or more specialized marksmen/women in your group is a good idea. These individuals can pick off lone zombies at long distances, and they are especially useful as a defensive measure against human bandits, who will likely be armed with guns and other weapons.

Sharpshooters, if you mean someone allocated the best long-range weapon, should be someone with the most experience shooting guns, especially rifles. Whether or not your sharpshooter is a soldier or a hunter, he or she should clearly be a good shot in order to get the job of sniper. Sharpshooters should help instruct other members of the group so that their weapon skills improve, time and resources permitting. This in general is true of any group member with useful knowledge. Share with the group, and you will be more likely to survive in the long run.

Sharpshooters should obviously have a weapon useful at delivering fire at long ranges. Bolt-action or assault rifles equipped with scopes are ideal for this role. You won't be firing at the extreme distances of military snipers engaged in conventional warfare, because your main enemy is the zombie. But you still need accuracy at range. A specialized weapon useful for the sharpshooter is a suppressed .22 rifle. These are very quiet with the suppressor attached and ammunition is plentiful. They won't be effective at the ranges that larger calibers are, so don't expect your .22 to have the same effectiveness as an M4/AR-15 rifle in terms of penetration, but at shorter ranges they are quite effective.

If manpower permits you should provide a spotter for your sharpshooter, more to help watch the sniper's back than to help him or her check the effectiveness of fire downrange. Scouts would be ideal for this role, and they can position themselves to relay information between the front lines and the rest of the group farther back.

Sharpshooters working against zombies have a different task than those dealing with human enemies. Zombies have no officers or chain of command to disrupt, so you won't be sowing confusion and fear in the enemy ranks. What you will be doing is helping to thin an advancing horde before it makes contact with your friends in the rest of the group. Sharpshooters should position themselves in locations where height or some indestructible barrier helps defend them against the undead. From there they can pour fire into an advancing band of zombies and be in a position to relay information to the rest of their group. If the sharpshooter has a suppressed weapon, whether this is a .22LR rifle or an M4, he or she is in a position to silently eliminate zombies without them advancing in the direction of fire. It may even be possible for a well-placed and properly equipped sharpshooter to eliminate an entire band of zombies by him or herself, given sufficient ammunition.

The Soldier- I've said repeatedly above that in the apocalypse everyone will need to become a warrior. That said, if you're part of a large enough group where you can afford such things, specialization is not a bad idea. While everyone has to be able to participate in combat, if you've got the manpower to be picky then as above certain roles should be filled with certain qualified people. Soldiers, as I understand them here, should be capable of and equipped for close combat against the undead. They should also be able to take part in a firing line and be effective out to intermediate ranges. In order to fulfill these requirements, equipment needs to be carefully considered, as does the physical demands of the job.

Soldiers need to be physically capable of close combat with zombies. That means they need to be able to swing an axe or a sword for an extended period of time, while carrying the weight of partial armor and other weapons and equipment. This is not a gender-specific requirement—I've met women who would be more than capable of swinging an axe, and a lot of men who wouldn't be. Both the individual and other group members need to be honest with themselves about who does what duty. The thirteen-year-old student and the hundred-and-five pound former secretary shouldn't get selected to be on the kickball team, as it were. Pick strong people who are in reasonable physical shape. Zombies are strong, and if you're going to be effective at close range you'll need muscles of your own.

Soldiers should form the main battle line of your post-apocalyptic army. Think of them as being analogous to the grenadiers of a Napoleonic army, who were meant to engage in extended firefights at close range and attack enemies at bayonet-point. Soldiers should be expected to fulfill the same role against the regiments of the undead, firing on them at close range and cutting them down with hand weapons. In order to accomplish that task, soldiers should be armed with the appropriate equipment.

In terms of weaponry they should have firearms and extra ammunition, as well as some form of powerful hand weapon. As above, magazine-fed guns are useless once their magazines are empty. So a soldier should be armed with whichever firearms are available that <u>also</u> have extra magazines. AR-15/M4-style assault rifles are excellent choices for the soldier, due to the nearly universal compatibility of their magazines. The rounds for these weapons, 5.56mm NATO, are small and light enough for a soldier to carry lots of extra ammunition. If you don't have access to these, another excellent (but shorter ranged) choice would be a Glock pistol in 9mm, again because of the availability of extra magazines. Soldiers will need to be able to keep up a steady rate of fire for extended periods of time, carefully squeezing off aimed shots in succession.

Firearms should obviously be supplemented with hand weapons, and soldiers should be carrying a serious weapon, not just a knife or two. Soldiers may need to engage in offensive close combat with the undead, and so your thinking should take you back to the medieval past—maces, swords, axes and other heavy weapons are the weapons of the soldier. These are backup weapons, but think of them differently than you would the combat knife on your belt. That is a last-ditch means of making an escape, not something you're intending to use in a close-range assault. A soldier should be armed with a dedicated hand weapon that will reliably slash through or crush a zombie skull. Whether these are handmade or modified implements or reproduction medieval weapons, they need to be capable of real combat.

Soldiers, especially if they're intending to get into close combat, should wear some sort of body armor. This doesn't have to be a full mail hauberk or a shark suit—it should be something sufficient to make close combat safer for the soldier, increasing his or her survivability, and remain light enough not to cause exhaustion. As I mentioned above it is my opinion that armor can and should be manufactured, and it should be targeted to protect those parts of the body most likely to be exposed to zombie bites. They're not going to go after your ankles, after all—they're going to direct bites at the face and neck, the shoulders and the forearms. So a soldier who wants to get medieval with the dead hordes should be thinking about ways to armor some or all of those locations.

One possible package of equipment (among myriad possibilities) would be to have your soldier armor his forearms and wear a leather jacket or flak vest, to provide partial armor. Following this the individual would carry a Glock 17 9mm and four extra magazines, giving him or her a total of 68 rounds of ammunition quickly available. Lashed to the soldier's belt beside these magazines should be a combat knife with at least a seven-inch blade and a war axe (which started life as a tool in a hardware store). This equipment is not so heavy that the soldier will quickly tire, and it allows him or her the ability to engage zombies at range and up close with great effectiveness.

Soldiers should support one another in combat. This means watching each other's backs and flanks and working together to maintain a steady rate of fire. Like Napoleonic infantry soldiers the goal is to keep up a rapid rate of fire while maintaining some semblance of accuracy. Don't blaze away as fast as you can. It might be reassuring (it was in Napoleon's time too), but you can't afford to waste your ammunition. Try as much as possible to make every shot count.

The Engineer/Armorer- Another group of skills that are incredibly important are those having to do with making or fixing stuff. The "stuff" I'm referring to is anything material that is useful or usable by the group. There aren't going to be any corner mechanics in the apocalypse. Anything that needs to be repaired or manufactured has to be manipulated by the members of the group. And while most people in the US have some rudimentary skill with tools and knowledge of basic repair, anything sophisticated or complex needs a specialist.

Everything that you make use of in the apocalypse will have to be maintained, and people who know the requisite skills are valuable. In our current society mechanics have fairly low status— but after civilization collapses they will suddenly become important people. The difference between a medieval existence and something that at least approximates civilization will be the people who know how to fix things.

Cars, for example, are crucial for any zompocalyptic war effort. They can be used as weapons. They are important for the gathering and transportation of supplies. They are also highly useful as a means of escape, which you should expect to be doing a lot. The problem with these vehicles is that they require maintenance or they'll break down. Thus the individual who knows how to maintain them and jury-rig available materials to keep them running is an important part of your group.

Weapons must also be maintained. Daily maintenance isn't so difficult, but ask the average office worker to field strip an AR-15 or a 1911A1 and you'll have a puzzle on your hands. People who were either trained gunsmiths or serious private gun owners (or soldiers, etc.) should be pressed into service as armorers. As with any specialized individual they should share their knowledge with others, even as they make use of their abilities in a "professional" capacity.

If you have any hope of maintaining electricity and all the boons that go with it, you're going to need someone who understands wiring and alternative means of power generation. Whether this is makeshift solar, wind, or water power, if you want to live like it's 1910 you'll need somebody to build and maintain your miniature power grid.

While this might seem peripheral to a discussion of weapons and warfare, I assure it is not—maintaining morale is extremely important, and a little bit of electricity will provide some of the conveniences to make it easier to do this.

"Poor little boy, all alone, no friends..."

My amazing fifth-grade teacher had a tendency to use the above phrase in a variety of situations, many of which were humorous. I use it here in a very different context, in regards to being all by your lonesome in a changed world. While groups of survivors might organize themselves as an army—and they should—a lone individual is going to have to fulfill all the tasks of a group of survivors by him or herself. This is not as grim as it might sound. There are possibilities available to a lone individual that become more difficult for a group of people. Just the same, a group has capabilities that the loner does not.

If you're by yourself, you'll need to be an army (of one, if you believe in the US Army's tagline). This isn't quite as stupid as it sounds, but you'll need to carefully gauge your strengths and weaknesses in regards to combat. Avoid, obviously, tangling with large groups. You can't fight a whole band by yourself. You most definitely should not charge into close combat with a horde of zombies. Doing so is a good way to meet a greasy and painful death. This is all the more true of smaller or physically weaker survivors. If you aren't good at pretending to be a Viking berserker, then avoid jumping into an axe-fight with fifteen zombies.

As a lone survivor, you'll be in a position to travel quietly. This is good because you won't be able to fight off large groups of zombies or an entire band of bandits by yourself. When you're alone, silence and discretion are your allies. If you have to pick and choose from the skill sets of the "classes" laid out above, you'll want to be more scout and sharpshooter than warrior. You should obviously equip yourself for the possibility of close combat, so arm yourself with at least a large knife. But going hand-to-hand with anything more than one or two zombies at a time is something to be avoided like the plague. You know that part in most action movies where the hero (or heroine) goes kung-fu on a host of bad guys and wipes the floor with them? Yeah, that's not real life. In real life when one guy starts a bar fight with eight other guys, he gets hospitalized. And that's getting off light. If you lose a fight with eight zombies, they'll celebrate their victory by eating you while you watch. Don't attack groups.

Sleeping needs to be carefully considered when you're by yourself. With nobody to stand watch, you're at the potential mercy of whatever creatures come across you while you're snoozing. Zombies, of course, don't have mercy and you'll awaken to the sounds and smells of them beginning to eat you. Bandits might also not have any mercy with them at the moment, and you could find yourself enslaved, put on the menu (if they're cannibals...you never know) or some other similarly nasty fate. At the very least they might think it amusing to rob you of your equipment and send you without shoes or weapons into the zombie-infested wilderness. In order to avoid any of these setbacks, you should pick and choose very carefully where you end up sleeping. Any place that is hidden or lockable is better than a place that isn't. Stay invisible, stay quiet, and find a temporary fortress. If you have to sleep locked in the trunk of car, then better than sitting by your cook fire in unknown territory waiting for whatever might come your way. Remember that without the noise of industrial civilization it will be relatively easy to hear other people, and easier for other people to hear you. Stay quiet. The light and smoke of fires is also something to carefully consider. You'll be able to smell and see the fires of other people, just as much as they'll make note of yours. Don't broadcast your presence to other humans who may be less than friendly. Even relatively normal people are bound to be jumpy and trigger-happy. Groups who've given themselves over to raping and pillaging are much more dangerous, and you don't want to tangle with them by yourself.

Make sure you carry some medical supplies with you if you're alone. There won't be a medic to patch you up if you cut yourself on glass or twisted metal. Make sure to keep wounds clean and always carry some form of disinfectant. Shoes and socks are a crucial part of your equipment, so make sure you pay attention to them. Change your socks regularly and let your feet breathe when you get the chance. With damaged feet you'll have a hard time running away, and you'll need to do that often. So take care of your feet. They are your first line of defense. While you're paying attention to your feet, make sure that you have decent shoes. Hiking boots or even snake-proof boots are good choices. Ditch the heels and the trendy loafers. You need to fight and run and march, so make sure the shoes you wear are capable of these things.

As a loner your weaponry should be well chosen and practical. Weight is more of a consideration that it is with a group of people based at a secure location. If you're wandering about you'll want to make sure that your weapons are light and effective. Keep them clean and in good condition. Hand-to-hand combat against lone zombies is important for a single survivor, since you want to stay as quiet as possible. Don't waste loud bullets on the one zombie you encounter feeding on a dead motorist. Use a knife, axe or sword instead, it's quieter. Against lone zombies you should pretend that you're a ninja on an assassination mission. Sneak up behind and do your business, and get out. Don't announce your lineage like medieval warriors ("I am Tim, son of Chuck.."). Keep it quiet.

Guns should be chosen (if there's a choice to be had) with all of the recommendations above in mind. Light weight and portable are the key words. Ammunition should be light weight, and you should ideally find something with several magazines. If you can find something with a silencer, all the better. The key to living to fight another day as a single individual is staying quiet and invisible.

When encountering other groups of people, take care to scout them out first. Watch how they interact with each other and try to discern their overall demeanor. If they do laundry like people before the apocalypse, they're probably safer than a group of people who wear war paint and decorate their camp with severed heads.

The Field Battle

Real battle against the undead is different than single combat or skirmishes with small groups of zombies. By "field battle" I mean a determined, prolonged engagement against a considerable body of undead enemies, with the goal of wiping them out to the, err, last man. This is obviously a dangerous undertaking that will utilize all your survival skills. The payoff for a successful battle will be a temporary reprieve from danger (or at least a lessening of it), as well as access to material resources that were previously too dangerous to obtain (because of the zombies).

Preparation is the key to winning a large-scale conflict with the undead. In a very real sense a battle should already be won by the time it starts. Careful planning will let your group dictate the course of events—after all, zombies are nothing if not predictable, so you're not going to have to respond to novel tactics on their part. Zombies always launch frontal assaults with whatever numbers they have. The main danger is that the undead will almost certainly outnumber you in every encounter, so a bit of careful calculation is required on your part if you want to be successful as a post-apocalyptic general. Again, the course of events of a battle fought against zombies is not the same as a modern conflict between twenty-first century armies. Your inspiration, instead, should be drawn from an amalgam of Napoleonic and medieval military history. Allow me to explain below.

The first thing that you'll want to know is information about the enemy force you'll be facing. Napoleonic armies didn't have sophisticated satellite networks and spy planes to help them gather information about an opposing force. They had to go out and look for themselves—or rather their light cavalry scouts had to go out and look, and report back about what they found. So in order to understand what you might be up against, you'll want to dispatch scouts to reconnoiter the ground ahead. As they go scouts should take note of the terrain features, whether natural or manmade, that might be of use in the context of a full-scale battle. Are there buildings that will act to restrict enemy movements, or funnel the undead in one direction or another? Are there impassable fences, ditches, gorges or walls that will deny your zombie enemies movement in one or more directions? Are their open areas where zombies can come at your group from several locations? Are you in danger of being outflanked, and if so where? Good scouts will note all of these things, and be able to provide a set of detailed instructions to the group (or the commander) so that a battle plan can be formulated.

In Napoleonic times light cavalry, the eyes and ears of an army, carried notebooks and pencils with them as a regular part of their equipment. They used these to write messages, but also to draw simple maps and make notes about what they saw. It would be a good idea for post-apocalyptic scouts to follow the example of these cavalrymen, and carry their own notebooks.

The other primary duty of scouts is to determine the location and disposition of enemy forces. Most of time this will mean asking "how many zombies are there?" and "how far away are they?" This is obviously not an exact science. Military history is littered with examples of scouts making wild errors in their estimation of enemy numbers. We're just not that good, especially under the influence of stress, at looking at a large group of individuals and guessing how many might be there. Binoculars should be used to help determine enemy numbers, but care should be taken by the scout to ensure that he or she remains hidden. You want to engage zombies on your own terms, on terrain of your choosing, and that means the enemy force shouldn't be provoked into attacking until all your preparations have been made. Scouts should do their best to estimate enemy numbers, but it is of the utmost importance that they remain hidden and silent whist they accomplish that task. When you go about deciding who should be a scout, make sure you select calm individuals, rather than the half-crazed biker who always wants to start a fight. Stay hidden, gather information, and get back to the group.

When the scouts have finished their analysis of relevant terrain features and the strength of the enemy, they should fall back silently and report to the group. At that point preparations for battle can be made. The process of provoking a battle against zombies owes a lot more to ancient warfare than it does to modern conflicts between twenty-first century armies. Modern battlefields spread over vast areas, and long-ranged weapons means that soldiers control large swathes of territory to their front. Mechanization and aircraft (and numerous other modern inventions) mean that a commander can attack an opponent whether or not the opposing force is ready. This scenario is quite a bit different from what happened in the ancient world.

Ancient armies could really only engage in battle if both sides agreed to fight. If one or the other force decided they didn't want to risk it, then they could simply march in the opposite direction. Few armies were fast enough to catch an opponent and force battle. This is one of the reasons why large-scale field battles were so rare—essentially both sides had to be convinced that they would win. If one side was clearly perceived as superior, then battle was unlikely. Even in Napoleonic times armies generally engaged in more or less the same way—battlefields were small, and the less confident side had the advantage of choosing ideal terrain to defend. The attackers had the harder job of dislodging their opponents from positions that were (ideally) selected to make them hard to attack.

Battle fought against the undead should generally follow the ancient pattern. Scouting should determine the number and location of opponents, and once that information is relayed preparations can be made to provoke combat. Since zombies always attack once they perceive living humans, you'll always be fighting on the defensive. This puts you in the same position as the Duke of Wellington, who defeated the French at Waterloo in 1815—Wellington himself more or less always fought from the defensive, provoking his opponents to attack him on ground of his choosing. Whereas Wellington had to goad enemies into doing this (or at least hope they were aggressive enough to do it on their own), you have the advantage of facing a predictable and single-minded opponent who will always launch a frontal assault.

If your scouts have done their jobs correctly and remained hidden, the band of zombies you mean to destroy will remain ignorant of your location. With the knowledge of how many they are and where they are, you (or whoever is in command) can prepare to fight them. One of the first actions you take should be to anchor the flanks of your army on impassible terrain, as ancient armies would. Through the time of Napoleon battlefields were more or less compact, and armies took great pains to ensure that their vulnerable flanks were secure. They could be made safe with mobile forces, especially horsemen, put there to guard them. Your post-apocalyptic survivor army won't have that as an option, and so you'll need to take the precaution of an all-infantry force and use terrain or entrenchment to defend your flanks. You want your predictable zombies predictably attacking you from only one direction. Buildings and other man-made structure can be ideal for blocking access to attacking zombies. You can also utilize entrenchment (of a sort), modifying available terrain features and structures to further restrict undead movements. Barbed wire can be used in this way, tied between trees and light posts and anywhere else you can attach it to provide a temporary barrier impassible to zombies. Large vehicles can also be used to block and restrict enemy movements—zombies aren't smart and so blocking off an alleyway with a bus is going to stymie them. Bridges and staircases are also useful terrain features to utilize in your war against the undead. Wherever you decide to position your battle line, it should be a place that forces the zombie horde to come at you from one direction, in a predictable (and planned for) frontal assault. Launching yourself and your friends into a spontaneous gunfight with unknown numbers of zombies is an excellent way to get outflanked, surrounded, and devoured. Don't be George Armstrong Custer and just charge in. His reward was being massacred by lots of angry Sioux warriors. And he wasn't anywhere near as outnumbered as you will potentially be.

Once you've chosen an appropriate piece of ground to defend, you'll want to place any sharpshooters you have in good firing positions and form your battle line. Sharpshooters should ideally be placed somewhere elevated, giving them a better line of sight and allowing them to update your knowledge of enemy numbers and movements as events unfold. The job of the sharpshooter isn't only to thin the ranks of advancing corpses—it is also the observation of the enemy and any reinforcements they might be getting from beyond your line of site from the ground. Sharpshooters should be ready to make the decision to break contact with the enemy and flee. If you risk being overwhelmed, then orders need to be given to retreat before you risk annihilation.

The main body of your force should be formed in a battle line, a miniature version of the basic formation of both ancient and Napoleonic infantry. There's no need to take cover against zombies, as they won't be returning your fire. They're specialized shock infantry, as you recall. In order to repel them you should form a relatively loose firing line with good lines of sight to the front of the formation. Warriors in the line of battle should be armed with both missile weapons (ideally firearms) and hand weapons for close combat. Those in the line of battle will be expect to pour a steady and accurate stream of fire upon advancing zombies in order to cut them down as they approach.

Always allow for a reserve to be ready to support the warriors in your main line of battle. The concept of keeping a reserve is relatively ancient (depending on how you define it, of course). The Roman legions, for example, customarily fought in a formation that included multiple supporting lines of infantry. Thus fresh troops from the rear ranks would always be available to reinforce the front lines, or maneuver to deal with unexpected threats. By Napoleon's time the growing sophistication of military forces saw army reserves increase in importance until they were the mechanism that often decided battles. Napoleon (and his enemies, as they learned from their mistakes) usually used a picked force of assault troops that were kept out of the main line of battle until a point of climax had been reached. Once he determined that the time had come, artillery would weaken a point in the enemy line, which would then be attacked by these reserves. As the period went on, history began to show that army that was the last to commit its remaining reserves would likely win. Against a horde of zombies, you should always maintain a reserve (even if it is only a single individual), for a number of reasons.

One reason for holding a reserve is that they can be used defensively. If you've missed a hole in the fence to your right and zombies start to outflank you, then the reserve element of your army should be used to deal with this threat. Always watch your back. People serving as reserves should keep one eye on what their allies are doing and one eye on everything else they're <u>not</u> paying attention to. Properly set up, a single survivor should be able to destroy many zombies. To a certain point of view, at least abstractly, you owe it to the remnants of the human race to destroy as many zombies as you can. There is no excuse for being killed by a single individual just because nobody was keeping an eye out.

Once your preparations are complete you should provoke your zombie opponents to battle you. This is straightforward, since zombies will launch a single-minded assault at any human they perceive. Scouts should use noise to draw zombies towards them, and then these will act to draw others. Once the firing starts you won't have to worry about attracting any nearby zombies to your position. Note that zombies have a tendency to follow one another, so that if a single zombie or a small handful are drawn towards you then others will surely follow. Once the attack begins everyone should fall back to their places in or near the battle line so that they can support one another.

As the zombie horde approaches your line any sharpshooters you have in position should try to thin their ranks as fast as possible. This should not be indiscriminate. Sharpshooters are not firing at random only to drop a certain number of the undead—when I say that they should thin the enemy ranks as they approach, I mean it quite literally. Dozens of zombies massed close together in a sort of unwitting phalanx are more dangerous than those that are spread out. Hand to hand combat is impossible if your undead foes are tightly packed—you simply won't be able to cut them down fast enough to avoid being overwhelmed. So the job of the sharpshooter is to target close-packed groups of zombies and pick off individual members of the group in order to break up their formation. Explosives, if available, may serve to accomplish the same thing. You won't destroy the undead, but you will shove them around and knock them down. Anything that forces them to come at you one at a time is something you'll want to consider.

Once the front ranks of the undead army reaches effective firing range (which will vary depending upon the skills and weapons deployed by you and your allies) you should commence firing. The goal is to maintain a steady and accurate fire. Don't lose your head and fire so rapidly that your accuracy declines. Try to make every bullet count. As the group in the firing line blazes away, anyone placed in reserve should be ready to take their place. This is another one of the main uses of holding some form of reserve—namely that they can relieve one of their comrades when he or she empties their gun or their last magazine. Remember that you might not be in the position of a well-provisioned military unit with lots of M4 rifles and ample spare magazines. A motley collection of scavenged firearms in various calibers is more likely what you'll have available. Many won't have more than one extra magazine. Some won't have any at all. This means that in order to maintain a steady rate of fire you'll have to have some part of your force waiting with a loaded weapon so they can relieve anyone who runs out of ammunition. People can be fed from your reserve into the line of battle and maintain a more or less constant fire upon your zombified enemies. Those stepping out of the line of battle should keep an eye on their surroundings and reload, waiting to jump back into the firing line. This basic formula for organizing a line of battle owes a lot more to Napoleonic warfare than it does modern twenty-first century battle practices, but against zombies it will be capable of cutting down even fairly large groups. If any zombies close to within contact distances, each member of the battle line should be able to fight them off with hand weapons. This is even more crucial if your ammunition supplies aren't as healthy as they should be. Note, as I've stressed above, that hand to hand combat is dangerous and needs to be carefully considered.

There are two outcomes to the hypothetical battle plan as I've outlined it above. One is that you and your group win a victory by cutting down all of the zombies opposing you. The immediate vicinity at least will temporarily be devoid of enemies, and so you can relax to a certain extent. The other outcome is that despite your efforts you are unable to halt the advance of the dead. At some point the decision needs to be made to flee, if you perceive that you'll be unable to stop the zombies in front of you. Perhaps your scouting efforts failed to be as accurate as you had hoped. Perhaps the attacking zombies started to receive reinforcements from the surrounding countryside faster than you could put them down. Whatever the reason, if the tide turns against you, you and your group will need to make a hasty getaway.

Breaking contact—retreat, fleeing, running away—is always something you should consider before a situation gets out of hand. Caution is the better part of valor. As you abandon your position you should do so in an orderly fashion, with a rear-guard helping to slow up the zombies who will now be pursuing you. Vehicles or obstructing terrain features should have been placed in order to allow you to make a clean getaway. The importance of an orderly retreat is difficult to overstate. Whatever you do, don't panic and run. Keep everyone together and make sure no one gets left behind. Panicking is a good way to get separated from your group and trapped. It also puts other group members in danger. With your people at a safe distance from the undead you can regroup and plan your next movements. The goal, as always, is to live to fight another day.

Individual and Small-Group Combat

All survivors should be prepared to fight zombies one on one. In fact, such opportunities, if they are slightly controlled, are an excellent way of gaining battle experience. Learning how to fight a lone zombie can be used as a means of gaining the skills needed to survive larger battles against greater odds. It is also relatively safe, as long as you exercise a certain degree of caution.

Zombies are not fast or agile. Their coordination is sufficient to propel them forward and not much beyond that. In particular, zombies are vulnerable to being outflanked in a fight. They don't have the physical coordination needed to turn rapidly. What this means is that in a fight with a zombie you should take advantage of their weakness by circling around them. If you move rapidly to the side of your zombie, it will need to turn to face you before it can move forward again. Where a human opponent would see you telegraph your movement and intercept you, a zombie has no choice but to halt and turn to face you again. In that short span of time that the zombie is readjusting its footing, slice off or crush its head. You are much faster than a zombie, and you should take every opportunity to exploit this in battle.

A single zombie is not that dangerous, at least as long as the person facing it has some idea of how to deal with it. Panicked individuals in the initial stages of society's collapse most likely will have ended up on the menu of many a lone zombie. If you keep your head about you and know what to do a single walking corpse is more target practice than threat. Your speed and intelligence should more than trump the strengths of the zombie, if you only have to face one a time. So take advantage of this and train yourself for combat.

Close combat with hand weapons should be practiced first against single zombies. Bring a friend, if you have one, and then you'll have someone to watch your back. Against zombies speed is more important than technique. In a sword fight with a human you'd need to know all sorts of blocks and feints and train to read the body language of your opponent. But zombies wouldn't recognize a feint even if you used one against them. So what you'll need to practice are fast, accurate blows aimed at the head. With swords and other edged weapons slightly more skill is needed than with weapons like maces or clubs. This is because cutting weapons (perhaps swords especially) need to land accurately with their blades in proper alignment. If you swing a sword through the air you can actually feel the difference between a correct alignment of the blade and a stroke where the alignment is off. If your sword blade hits squarely on the point of impact it will cut. If the blade is twisted to one side as the blow lands it will likely roll off the target and fail to bite. Practice makes perfect, so you should practice cutting with your sword (ideally on lone zombies) until proper technique and blade alignment is instinctive.

Even if you have a "favorite" weapon you should practice with everything you have available. You might lose or break your special sword, axe or gun—so be prepared to improvise. Learn how to use a variety of weapons and practice with all of them. The end result of your battle practice is to make you a jack-of-all-trades (and hopefully a master-of-all-trades, should you manage to survive long enough). A properly trained warrior should be able to use whatever weapon is at hand.

In small groups zombies are more dangerous than as single individuals, but still nowhere near as deadly as they are in greater numbers. Joining battle with a small group of zombies should be done according to the composition of a party of survivors and the available weaponry.

Lone survivors should use caution if they are too outnumbered. If there are too many zombies or they're too closely packed you should avoid close combat and use missile weapons instead. If you have something silent (ideally a suppressed .22 caliber pistol or rifle) then you may be able to deal with your enemies without them being able to respond. If you don't have a silent option then you should consider carefully if it is worth it or not to attack them. Will your gunfire draw in more zombies from the surrounding area? Do you have any idea of how many the undead are in your immediate vicinity? Do you have enough ammunition if you need to defend yourself against a sustained attack? Do you have an escape route if things begin to go badly? When by yourself you should always practice caution.

A group of survivors, even if this is only a pair of individuals, has a better chance of surviving skirmishes with the undead. You and your friend or friends have the ability to plan and take precautions to defend each other and watch for ambushes. The zombies don't have this. The same considerations apply—how much ammunition, how many zombies, escape routes and so on. But if you have backup and the numbers aren't too heavily stacked against you, you should be able to fight and win.

A group of survivors engaging in close combat need to take their inspiration from the professional armies of the ancient world. The Romans are an ideal model to use in this respect. Wild melees with everyone pairing off to fight at random have more to do with Hollywood's conception of ancient warfare than they do with reality. Ancient armies, even poorly organized ones, uniformly fought in a variety of close formations. The reasons for this are both practical and psychological. In practical terms a close formation allows each member of that formation to defend and be defended by the people next to him (or her). The goal of ancient infantry warfare was based around keeping the enemy <u>out</u> of your formation while trying to break into his. One of the dividends of this is that you don't have to worry about someone attacking you from your sides or rear. They have to come at you straight on, where you can see them and fight back. In the realm of human psychology a close fighting formation reassured everyone that they weren't alone, that they had someone right next to them you could fight with them. This made everybody a better fighter, more able to stand the mental strains and terror of battle. Both aspects of a close fighting formation are crucial to survivors engaging in close combat with the undead.

Don't break your fighting formation. Like the Romans, you should stay near your comrades and cut down enemies that come into your danger zone. Don't run all over the battlefield like an action hero, because you're exposing yourself— stupidly—and endangering the other members of your group. Sufficient distance should be maintained in a formation for everyone to use their weapons safely (don't gouge out your neighbor's eye as you draw your machete back, it's bad form). Other than that you should remain close to one another and make sure zombies don't break into your formation.

Bandits and Survivors

Your fellow humans can be a blessing or a curse. Strength exists in numbers, as in warfare ancient and modern, but telling who is friend and foe will be a crucial (and difficult) task in the zompocalypse. In crisis situations humans demonstrate both good and bad qualities. Sometimes disaster brings out the best in people. Too often it brings out the very worst. With civilization gone and family members scattered or dead, many of the people you encounter will be reduced to the point where they would kill for the bare essentials of survival. That can of beans you've got might be enough for someone else to try and take your life. More disturbing are people whose inner nature takes a turn for the dark with the restrictions of modern society washed away. You can and will encounter "people" for whom killing and stealing and raping is a part of their new life. The apocalypse is a time to be untrusting of strangers, for many of them will be "people" in only the loosest of terms.

This is not to say that everyone will have abandoned all hope, and with it the vestiges of what made them human. Truly evil people are rare, even in the apocalypse, but their actions might outweigh their relatively small numbers. Many of the individuals and groups you encounter will be like you, maybe hungry, desperate and afraid but still human. Like you they won't find pleasure in cruelty. They won't see the other remnants of humanity as resources to be used for gain or pleasure. But there are some who will.

Those who live their post-apocalyptic lives as predatory raiders I choose to term "bandits." There are many other terms you might use—Viking, brigand, pirate—but bandit, for me, captures the essence of what I mean to describe in human predators. In the ancient world bandits were a scourge. They were plunderers and thieves and slavers, living off the suffering of other people. Bandits were hated by city-states and settled folk, and the punishments for banditry were draconian. Be captured as a bandit by the Romans of a certain time, and you'd find yourself "fed" to the machine of the arena, to be slaughtered spectacularly by gladiators or wild beasts, dying to the cacophony of the countless thousands in the crowds above. Bandits were hated, and with good reason.

Human survivors will be dangerous to you in ways that zombies will not be. This is because other humans potentially have the same skills that you do. If you're lucky they won't have read this volume, or the other works covering the topic of apocalyptic survival. Maybe they haven't read Che Guevuara's book on guerilla warfare. They might not be ex-soldiers with combat experience. But then again they might be. Maybe like you they read useful material about survival and took the lessons to heart. Maybe they're as dangerous as you've taught yourself to be.

Humans represent a danger that is potentially more sudden than that posed by zombies. Zombies react slowly, and are dangerous in numbers, especially large numbers. In contrast, while you won't likely encounter many other survivors, those you do run across are likely to be very dangerous to you. Humans (potentially) have firearms, like you (probably) should. They can inflict lethal injuries on you from a distance with these weapons, and they can attack before you know they're there. Remember, as mentioned repeatedly above, without medical care even fairly minor wounds can prove to be fatal. This is especially true of gunshot wounds, due to the way that bullets tend to crush and destroy tissue, in contrast to bladed weapons. They also tend to carry foreign material deep into wounds, which in the apocalypse will result in infection and eventual death. You don't want to risk being shot, and so humans armed with firearms are an especial danger. You should find a gun as soon as possible, in order to protect yourself against other humans with guns. This advice is especially important for denizens of the modern US, given the prevalence of firearms. The arms race has already been decided at the level of the individual, and guns will remain the deciding factor in post-apocalyptic warfare.

Human survivors are all the more dangerous because they can use their intact brains to form complex plans, a normally mundane thing that zombies cannot do. While zombies are eternally predictable, human opponents can do tricky things like place traps and ambushes for the unwary. They can and will attack you where or when they perceive you to be weak or off-guard. In order to survive against this threat, you will have to adjust your tactics accordingly.

Against humans, the ancient/Napoleonic model used through most of this volume is suddenly less applicable. You still won't be using the full toolset of modern warfare, due to the dependence of twenty-first century warfare upon technologies and machines that you won't have. But warfare directed against other survivors is nonetheless more modern in its inspiration than that aimed at the zombie horde.

The most likely model you should adopt draws its inspiration from the insurgent warfare of the mid-twentieth century. Faced with more powerful European enemies, insurgent groups adopted hit-and-run guerilla tactics, meant to slowly bleed the armies of their opponents. Major battle was not the goal. The purpose of guerilla warfare was attrition, a strategy of making warfare so long and expensive and pointless that an opponent would seek peace. Nations learned to counter these tactics in part by adopting some of their major elements, as with the American "Green Berets," the Special Forces troops who were developed to wage "asymmetrical" warfare against the Communist military forces in Vietnam. It is to these warriors, and their wars, that you should look when contemplating how to fight against human groups in the zompocalypse.

Much of guerilla warfare involves the techniques of surprise and ambush. If you're fighting against superior forces a surprise attack is always a good idea, and has been for millennia. Given the small numbers and insufficient medical care that will be the reality of post-apocalyptic warfare, you should always use every possible advantage at your disposal to ensure you minimize your casualties. You won't be able to easily replace losses to your group, so you need to take care to avoid taking them. Ambush allows you to inflict damage on an enemy group efficiently. Most survivors will not be professional military personnel with experience of combat, and so in this world of amateur warriors you should always try to fire first if you are forced to fight. Springing a successful ambush on an enemy or group of enemies will result in their death or flight. Most people won't have the training or psychological preparation to take cover and fire back effectively. Most people will run. So when you contemplate war against your fellow humans, you should always attempt to use your own ambushes and avoid those of others.

Critical to this goal is your ability to use intelligence information effectively. Whether as part of group or on your own you should always take care to scout out your surroundings. Pay careful attention to sound. Other humans will give away their presence with the sound of machinery or gunfire, the light of lamps or candles and the smoke from fires. You will also give your presence away in similar fashion, unless you take precautions to avoid being detected. Be cautious in unknown territory and take care not to give away your position. Dangerous groups of bandits are likely to be confident in their strength, and in consequence both noisy and overconfident. Make sure you pay attention to the sights and sounds around you to learn who else is lurking about.

Always save some of your bullets for defense against other humans. Bandits will likely have guns, and so you'll need your own in order to avoid death or enslavement. It is possible to fight zombies with only hand weapons, but against firearm-wielding bandits you won't be as effective armed only with a sword or spear.

If you do have to fight against human opponents, remember not to be squeamish. The injunctions against killing fellow humans will have vanished along with the rest of human society. Your enemies will in all likelihood show you know mercy, so you should return the favor. Shoot to kill. Leave no survivors who can give away your presence. This might seem cold, as a number of other bits of advice sprinkled throughout this text, but remember what this book is meant to do, and what it is not meant to do. I am not concerned here with the moral questions regarding the maintenance of some sort of abstract concept of humanity—the goal of this book is to prepare you to survive post-apocalyptic warfare. So act like a warrior and eliminate threatening humans. Bandits and other nefarious types are predators just as much as the zombies are, and you should eliminate them wherever you can. If destroying the undead is a public service to your fellow survivors, then destroying predatory looters and other human parasites is as well. I am not advocating the abandonment of all concepts of morality—on the contrary, honorable, "civilized" behavior is crucial to the survival of your group, since everyone needs to trust each other. But in combat, against opponents who would kill, torture, or enslave you, you should show no mercy.

Being captured by hostile humans may be a sort of worst case scenario, but even that can be planned for. For example, if you are thinking of such things, it might not be a bad idea to carry a knife or small handgun in an ankle holster. Most bandit types aren't going to frisk you like the cops might—after all, the police are trained and experienced "friskers" and so they do it out of habit and necessity. But post-apocalyptic thugs aren't probably going to look much beyond the obvious. Of course they may simply kill you immediately, but if they don't then a hidden weapon opens up possibilities you wouldn't otherwise have.

Not all human groups will be composed of dangerous marauders. You'll need to take care how you interact with everyone, so don't let your guard down, but some at least of your fellow human beings will be decent people who like you have retained bits of their underlying humanity. If you have the opportunity to forge good relations with

P a g e | **261**

other groups then you may be able to pool your resources and provide for mutual defense. If you're on your own you may have found a group of people worth joining, if they'll have you. There is strength in numbers, as always.

If you aren't interested in joining a group of survivors, there is still the possibility of peaceful exchange. And I mean "exchange" quite literally—in terms of trading. All of the dollars in your bank account and safe are useless to you once the society that utilized those things collapses. With the money economy gone, all exchange will revert to the barter system. This has obviously happened before, for example towards the end of the Roman Empire when trade in kind replaced the money economy that had flourished during Rome's prosperous centuries of expansion and domination. In the apocalypse only goods will be valuable, and so during your various foraging expeditions it might be wise to keep your eyes out for anything that could be potentially valuable to other people, and not just yourself. Food, shelter, ammunition, and other desirable things will all have a new price in the aftermath of the end of the world. While that price might vary it still no doubt exists. Quite likely the new society that emerges from the fall of the current one will forge new trade routes and reconstitute itself around a barter system where people buy and sell without the intermediary currency that we all tend to take for granted.

Your fellow humans represent, potentially, everything that is good and all that is bad. You'll have to be extremely cautious around them and use all of your judgment in dealing with them. If you have to fight them make sure you do so with determination and skill. If you happen to befriend them then you've taken a step forward in your continual struggle to survive. Find your friends and allies and keep them close, and despise all who would be a danger to you and yours.

The Ambush

Above I discussed how ambush is a key technique of what might be called "asymmetrical" warfare. It bears some further discussion, as this volume moves ever closer to its conclusion. But first, a case study in the techniques of the ambush.

Armies and armed war parties have been ambushing each other since the beginning of recorded history. Much of successful warfare is based around the manipulation of information. In an ambush, you don't want your opponent to be ready to fight you, and you want to inflict damage to him at a place and time of your choosing. Being able to accomplish this is tied inexorably to the use of intelligence information, which means you need to scout out your surroundings. Battles, ideally, are won before they begin. You want your opponent to have to react to you, and not the other way around.

The fall of civilization will have reduced the possibilities available to both you and your enemies. No longer are their aircraft and spy satellites and armored personnel carriers (well, hopefully, unless you're the one with the APC). Hostile humans will travel on foot or in/on civilian vehicles, for the most part. Horses and other draft animals are an outside possibility in some parts of the country, but we're focused here on vehicles. So—walking or riding, dangerous humans may want to harm you. Here's what you should do to improve your chances of survival.

First, note that both people and vehicles travel best along roadways. This is especially important for civilian cars, most of which aren't good at traversing broken terrain. So invading bandits will more than likely come at you along the "invasion routes" of local roads and highways. This means that you have some way of anticipating their movements. Map the area around your fortress, if you have one, and know the roads that lead in and out of the area. Vehicles will be much easier to hear, with industrial civilization gone. Control as much as you can the roadways that lead into and out of your home territory. If you expect attack, preparations should be made before the enemy arrives at your doorstep.

In order to stop an attacking force from quickly reaching you, you should use debris or barricades to shut off road access. Stakes, ditches and ruined cars are all readily available or easily manufactured. In forested regions tree trunks make excellent impassible barriers to motorized transport. Use spikes, nails or other debris to make caltrops to impede vehicles and unwary pedestrians. If an enemy intends to drive to your doorstep, make sure he can't get there.

Roadblocks of various kinds actually make excellent ambush points. Anything that forces a group of cars and trucks to stop is something that makes them easy prey for an ambush force. The techniques are quite simple, which is one of the reasons so many successful guerilla movements have adopted them in the last decades. Fire from prepared positions and use cover. Open your fire from several directions at once, to make it harder for your opponents to respond. Utilize explosives (there's a reason IEDs are used by guerilla forces) in order to demoralize and separate your enemies from one another. You'll get extra points for destroying/disabling the first and last vehicle in an enemy convoy. In the right terrain, this will trap the entire force along a roadway, where hopefully they'll be exposed to withering fire from your prepared positions. If you don't have the numbers to wipe out an enemy force, your aim should be to allow them enough room to escape, hopefully in a disorganized route which will help destroy their morale (something zombies don't have) and make them less likely to come back for another round.

If you want historical backing for the importance of ambushes, then look no farther than the Carthaginian general Hannibal Barca. Hannibal was a tricky opponent for the Romans during the Second Punic War (218-202 BCE), and inflicted a number of catastrophic defeats on them. The most famous of these is the battle of Cannae, in 216 BCE, where Hannibal destroyed a Roman army that greatly outnumbered him. Before that however, he launched one of the most successful ambushes in all military history at the Battle of Lake Trasimene. As a Roman army snaked its way around the shores of the lake, they were unaware that Hannibal's entire force was deployed around them, many of them uphill along the forested slopes that hung above the lakeshore. They were unaware of his presence right up to the point where he closed off their line of march and charged downhill, driving them into the lake. It was more of a slaughter than a battle, and those members of the Roman vanguard who managed to cut their way free were later surrounded and captured. Hannibal won not because his men were better fighters, or because they had superior weapons. He didn't win because of superior numbers, because his was in all likelihood the smaller army. He won because he manipulated information—he knew where the Romans would go, and they had no clear idea of his location—and fear, panicking them to the point where no serious resistance could be made. If you want to use anyone as your model in the wars of the zompocalypse, then you should choose Hannibal Barca. There is a reason why military strategists and tacticians have studied his battles for over two thousand years. He knew how to handle his business.

The Horde

Inevitably you will encounter a mass of zombies so large that you won't be able to defeat it. Maybe you're alone, in which case one hundred undead is too much for you to handle. Maybe you're part of a survivor band with thirty warriors, yet you lack the bullets and manpower needed to defeat three thousand zombies. In the situation of a field battle, your option is simple and well known by this point—you run. But what if you can't run? What if you're trapped in your fortress and surrounded by a mass of the unliving, unable to break the ring around you?

The situation is not entirely hopeless, if you find yourself surrounded by a massive horde, provided you've taken certain precautions. Firstly, unless you've taken the advice above and either found or manufactured a secure fortification, you'll be devoured. You can survive a siege, as in medieval Europe, only if your fortress is stout enough to stymie the besieging force for a time. If you do have a secure fortification, you'll need to find a way to break out of your encirclement, unless you have enough stockpiled ammunition to methodically cut down your besiegers.

So what do you do if you're surrounded in a stout defensive location but you lack the resources to eliminate the attacking horde? You have two options (well, three really, but we're trying to avoid going out in a blaze of glory)—flight, however that may be achieved, or by having a relieving "army" draw off your attackers. Flight has been covered above, but it bears remembering that zombies are not clever or well-coordinated. Escape can take many forms, whether this involves you delving through sewer tunnels or jumping from rooftop to rooftop. Telephone poles and fire escapes and for that matter any vertical surface can be great allies, since zombies don't climb. But what if climbing is not an option? What if you really are surrounded and trapped, you ask? There is one precaution you can take that has the potential to be your salvation. This is getting help from outside your fortress, the "relief army" as I style it. What do I mean by this? Let us see.

Historically sieges usually carried on for long periods of time, because until the arrival of gunpowder and siege cannons most well-built fortresses were largely immune to attack. Most successful sieges ended when the garrison was near starvation and had no hope of aid from outside. They then surrendered. If they did this within a reasonable timeframe, the attackers usually would spare the garrison. Resistance beyond an acceptable point of honor often resulted in the massacre of the defenders. Sometimes besieging armies would run out of money or supplies and be forced to retire before they could take a fortress. Sometimes disease forced them to withdraw. But one of the best ways to get a besieging army to quit and go away was to threaten it with attack by another force outside the walls of the fortress. Risking being attacked from two directions while your army was spread out in siege lines was enough to make many commanders rethink their plans and beat a hasty retreat.

Zombies, obviously, don't have commanders and they won't quit their siege while anyone inside remains alive. But they can be drawn off from their assault if something else catches their eye. Thus the "relief army" in a zombie siege isn't going to scare them into retreat, but instead provide enough noise and movement to draw off some or all of the attacking force and send it in a new direction.

For this reason it is a very good idea not to mass all of your forces within one fortified point. Ancient city states were protected by walls, but they also utilized forts and towers at a distance from the city to help watch for enemies and provide more options for dealing with them if they came. A group of twenty or thirty survivors should have at least one or two individuals brave enough to serve as the "border guards" of the group's' territory. The scouts and sharpshooters are probably the ideal candidates for this role, since they're already experienced in working more or less on their own. These brave men and women should be armed and equipped for their task, and they should have some sort of fortified location of their own to keep them safe. Communication between the main fortress and outlying border posts will need (in all likelihood) to make use of ancient technologies— mirrors, signal flags, fires, flares, noise (gunshots) and so on. Border guards should remain close enough that they can communicate with the main group. Binoculars and telescopes can stretch this distance considerably, provided there is sufficient line of sight between two points.

The goal of the outlying guardpost(s) is to remain silent and watch for enemy movements. Men and women guarding your borders should be as quiet and inconspicuous as possible, because remaining invisible to human and undead opponents is the armor that will keep them safe (and allow them to keep the rest of the group safe). In the event that a large force of zombies encircles the main camp or fortress, then the people manning the guard posts should leap into action.

Zombies are drawn to noise and movement. The goal of border guards hoping to draw off a besieging undead horde should be to make enough noise and distracting movement that some or all of that horde is drawn off in a new direction. Defenders within the besieged fortress will want to cease firing (or anything else that makes noise) in order to help the outlying guards do their job. Anything that can be used to distract zombies from their siege should be employed to make this happen. Flares and fires offer the potential of noise and movement. Vehicles are even better, because they provide some protection to the guards as they attempt to redirect the zombie horde. Battery-operated CD/MP3 players or even alarm clocks can be used to fool zombies into attacking phantoms—zombies won't know the difference between recorded sounds and those made by real live humans. Essentially anything that gets some or all of the encircling force to break off the attack and move away from your allies is fair game.

At the point that the siege is broken you have to decide whether to remain or to relocate to a safer location. If your fortress seems compromised it might be a good idea to abandon it and look for another more secure location. If you feel confident that you can defend your fortress, then you have the option of staying in place. The point here is that having dispersed guard posts and people to guard them gives you options that you wouldn't otherwise have. Simply packing everybody into one site allows the undead to surround you with an unbreakable undead wall. If you can't break out of it, you've probably lost your battle. Even if the surrounding zombie horde can't get into your fortress, you'll eventually succumb to the scourge of the besieged—thirst and hunger. Defenses (as with fortresses themselves) should always be in-depth. As with everything else in this volume, the best weapon you have is your intellect. The clever and adaptable survivor is the one that will thrive in the apocalypse.

Afterward

There is an element of voyeurism behind the fantasy of a zombie apocalypse, I think. It has to do with the concept of getting close enough to danger and terror to be thrilled by it, without having to deal with the gruesome reality that lies beneath the surface. As with any notion of the apocalypse, the thought that all of what we associate with "the world" around us might vanish is a frightening one. It is darkly fascinating, and so it draws our gaze. Zombies, in the fantastical sense covered in this volume, are only stand-ins for the real terrors of the real world—the disease or climate change or world war that might really destroy civilization as we know it. We are simultaneously repelled by and drawn towards stories about the end of everything.

Zombies take the dark-fascination part a bit further, though—the destruction that they promise comes not at the hands of a dangerous foreign enemy, or climatic upheaval, but at those of our fellows. When civilization falls to the undead, the four horsemen of the apocalypse will be unleashed by people we knew. People we went to school with. People we gossiped with during lunch breaks. People, maybe, that we loved. The fascination with zombies is tied irretrievably to the personal nature of this specific brand of apocalypse.

For further reading on the subject of zombies, you probably already know the handful of popular books written about them. I have written this in part as a response to the existing literature, but I encourage the reader to delve further and make his or her mind up concerning was is useful (and entertaining) advice. Beyond books specifically devoted to zombies, I would encourage the reader to look into the various histories that I have touched upon in the pages above. There is much to learn through the study of the past.

For an analysis of medieval swordsmanship (yes, there were martial arts in Western Europe), a great place to start would be with *Medieval Swordsmanship: Illustrated Methods and Techniques*, by John Clements (Paladin, 1998). Clements offers a magnificent and detailed account of the actual workings of medieval swordplay (and the use of other weapons), demonstrated through clear text and wonderful diagrams and illustrations. If you had to select one work through which to learn the basics of medieval combat, you should look no farther. Hank Reinhardt's *The Book of Swords* (Baen, 2009) likewise offers much useful information about swords and their use, backed by the considerable expertise of the author.

For a more detailed and technical understanding of swords and their use, readers should refer to *The Sword in Anglo-Saxon England* by H.R. Ellis Davidson (Boydell, 1962). This supplies a more scientific understanding of swords and their metallurgy and construction, as well as their use in war.

For an eastern take on swordsmanship, an excellent source is *Mastering the Samurai Sword* by Cary Nemeroff (Tuttle, 2008). The book offers a step-by-step, illustrated approach to the basics behind using a Japanese sword. While nothing can fill in for the actual experience of hands-on training, Nemeroff's book comes shockingly close to offering a personal lesson in ken-jutsu.

For more a more general history of the art of war in the medieval world, there are many excellent books to choose from. For the general reader I would suggest *Knights* by Andrea Hopkins (Grange, 1990), and *Arms and Armor of the Medieval Knight* (Crescent, 1996). Both of these offer a basic overview of weaponry and warfare as it was practiced in the European Middle Ages. In particular they offer the general reader a good understanding of the construction and materials utilized in medieval body armor, and the weapons developed to counter it.

For readers more interested in learning about warfare in ancient Japan, I highly recommend *Secrets of the Samurai* by Oscar Ratti and Adele Westbrook (Castle, 1999). Comprehensive and well illustrated, *Secrets of the Samurai* contains lots of useful/interesting information about the weapons and warfare of medieval Japan.

There are many volumes dedicated to the history of ancient warfare. The multi-volume work of Hans Delbruck is quite old (the 3rd edition was published in 1920), but still contains lots of interesting insights into the history of war. Ignore what Wikipedia has to say about Delbruck's ancient history—his analysis was insightful and ahead of its time in many ways. The final volumes of Delbruck's opus take the subject all the way through the period of the Napoleonic Wars, and so they comprehensively cover much of the history that I touch on above. They are available in translation from the original German, but they are directed more towards academics than they are to general readers, so tread cautiously.

My personal favorite work on ancient warfare (at least in terms of a popular, non-academic book) is still John Warry's marvelous *Warfare in the Classical World* (U. of Oklahoma Press, 1980). Make sure you get the older edition, which contains the beautiful and incredibly accurate illustrations that so appealed to me when I was a boy. As a professional historian of Rome, I can say that at times Warry takes his source material too literally, but as a general survey (as Warry intended) *Warfare in the Classical World* is a magnificent book.

For warfare in the Napoleonic world I heartily recommend *The Battle* by Alessandro Barbero (Walker & Company, 2003). His book is a highly entertaining and very detailed account of the Battle of Waterloo (1815), written through what must have been painstaking research into primary documents, especially memoirs, letters and diary entries set down by the combatants themselves.

For more general histories of warfare, look to *A History of Warfare* by John Keegan (Vintage, 1993), and *A World History of Warfare*, by Archer, Ferris, Herwig and Travers (U. of Nebraska Press, 2003). These condense vast amounts of information about the history of warfare in its epic entirety, from the Neolithic period onwards.

In terms of an understanding of more modern types of war, I suggest a look at *Guerilla Warfare*, by Che Guevara (U. of Nebraska Press, 1985). Whatever your feelings about the man and his politics, Guevara had considerable first-hand knowledge of low-level "asymetrical" warfare, and many of his insights are quite interesting.

If you're curious about anything that I've raised in the pages above, I encourage you to investigate and expand your knowledge. My friend and former advisor Steven Johnstone likes to say that an academic is anyone who has what he calls "disciplined curiosity." The discipline part refers to the will to learn about something that peaks your interest. The internet in our increasingly modern age is a wonderful tool for delving into pretty much any subject you can conceive of—and so in large part there is no excuse for saying "I don't know." Go out and find the answer. Knowledge, both before and after the zombie apocalypse, is power.

The End

45071080R00161

Made in the USA
San Bernardino, CA
31 January 2017